ELLIS ISLAND

Written and Illustrated by
Mary Betik Trojacek

A story about the Czech immigrants and life on the farm in the 1930's and 1940's

© Copyright 2005 Mary Betik Trojacek.
All rights reserved. No part of this publication may be reproduced, stored in a retrieval system, or transmitted, in any form or by any means, electronic, mechanical, photocopying, recording, or otherwise, without the written prior permission of the author.

Note for Librarians: A cataloguing record for this book is available from Library and Archives Canada at www.collectionscanada.ca/amicus/index-e.html
ISBN 1-4120-3551-1

Offices in Canada, USA, Ireland and UK

Book sales for North America and international:
Trafford Publishing, 6E–2333 Government St.,
Victoria, BC V8T 4P4 CANADA
phone 250 383 6864 (toll-free 1 888 232 4444)
fax 250 383 6804; email to orders@trafford.com

Book sales in Europe:
Trafford Publishing (UK) Limited, 9 Park End Street, 2nd Floor
Oxford, UK OX1 1HH UNITED KINGDOM
phone +44 (0)1865 722 113 (local rate 0845 230 9601)
facsimile +44 (0)1865 722 868; info.uk@trafford.com

Order online at:
trafford.com/04-1379

10 9 8 7 6 5

Mary Betik Trojacek

Beyond Ellis Island
By
Mary Betik Trojacek

"About the Book"

This story touches on the lives of the Czech Immigrants who came to America at the turn of the century. When they got off the ship and walked America's soil, they saw no limits to their dreams. All they had to do was give of themselves and work, thus the fitting title for this book, "Beyond Ellis Island." The immigrants had visions and worked hard toward their goal of owning land. Most Czechs were farmers whose way of life was growing and picking cotton. The whole family effort was put into it and children grew up in the cotton patch.

As I chronicled this story, "newsy bits" of information were entered respective to the pertinent years leading up to and through The Depression and war years, giving one a broader scope of the times. A vivid description of a family of ten, living on a farm in the '30's and the '40's is presented in a humorous way and is sure to bring out a chuckle. This book is a collection of memories evolved from my reflections, recollections, perceptions, and impressions of what transpired during my formative years.

Anyone who has lived on a farm can relate to this book and may be able to picture himself or herself in many of the episodes featured . . . because "that's the way it was back when."

"Author's Note"

    This family history is not complete by any means. So much information has gone by the wayside and is missing. Like most history, it was there all the time and could have been obtained and preserved when I was young and while my grandparents were still in my midst. I do not remember my grandparents talking much about their life in the old country, their immigration, or their past. The topic of their conversations usually was about the weather, the crops, the price of cotton and what was in the future. At that time grandchildren did not realize the value of their ancestral history and were not interested enough to ask questions. And now, sad to say, the wealth of knowledge my grandparents or my parents had will never be shared. It is hoped that many readers will be inspired to write down what they already know about their roots. They are encouraged to ask questions and talk to grandpa and grandma to learn more about their heritage. They are encouraged to write down the information before it is lost. Heritage is a gift. In preserving it, tribute is paid to our ancestors who laid the foundation that expresses who we are and what we stand for. If heritage is not kindled and preserved, eventually it will go by the wayside and be lost forever.

    In writing about my family roots, I go back 100 years when my grandparents came to America and endured the harsh reality of resettlement; I focus on the trials and blessings of my Mom and Dad and capture scenes and scenarios of the 1930's and the 1940's . . . my growing up years.

    Values of love God and your neighbor, honesty, self-discipline, and the secrets of survival were integrated into the lives of my ancestors who viewed these qualities as the basis for character and integrity.

I honor and thank my immigrant families for whom they were and what they stood for. This book reflects their spirit. My hope is for anyone who reads it will be enlightened about the Czech heritage and the Czech descendants will be the proud bearers of a legacy which their early immigrants left for them.

Beyond Ellis Island

"About the Author"
Author's Biographical Note

Mary Betik Trojacek was born in 1929 in Ennis, Texas, one of ten children born to Joe and Frances Marusak Betik whose parents were Czech immigrants. Many Czechs lived in the Ennis community, and Mary grew up in an environment of Czech culture, heritage, and traditions. Her elementary education was in a 3-room country school where all the kids spoke Czech and then learned English.

Joe and Frances Betik were cotton farmers and their children grew up in the cotton patch. They did without during the depression years, and joined the patriotic movement during the war years. During this time, the military draft was in full force. People at home planted Victory gardens to ease the shortage of food, cleaned up trash piles and sent all scrap metal to the defense plants. Many commodities were rationed; folks saved everything, hoarded what they could or just did without.

This book describes how they created their own good times and as a result had some unusual and hilarious experiences, doing many things you wouldn't let your own kids do.

Mary grew up in the 1930's and the 1940's and lived without push-button gizmos and gadgets, and because of that has a greater appreciation for the simple things in life.

She is a retired Registered Nurse and her husband of 56 years is raising Registered Angus cattle. They have seven children and take

Mary Betik Trojacek

time to enjoy their children, grandchildren and great-grandchildren.

Beyond Ellis Island

DEDICATION

Dedicated to the memory of my immigrant families, and to my father and mother, Joe and Frances Bětik, who through their love, sacrifice, determination, and an abundance of common sense, molded me to be what I am. I like being Me.

Mary Betik Trojacek

ACKNOWLEDGMENT

I extend heart felt gratitude to my husband, Jerry, for his loving patience and support as I was gathering and compiling information, reading and writing it down. In the past five years there were many times he cooked his own supper and watched T.V. alone.

This book was written especially for our family: Donna and Larry Isom; Matthew and Jillian Isom; Gerald, Jamie, Lucas, Juliana and Gregory Isom; Gary and Karen Trojacek; Richard and Audrianna Trojacek; Shohn, April, Hannah, and Corbin Trojacek, and Lydia and Madiline Johnson; Aaron and Amanda Trojacek, and Graysen Wilson; Joan Trojacek; Mary Denise and Richard Bruce; Christopher, Kay and Austin Trojacek, and Christian Whiddon; Jeffrey, Melanie, Annie, and Adeline Trojacek; and . . . future additions.

It was because of their encouragement that I wrote this book. They wanted to know how things were in the days when I was growing up, so, as I reminisced about the days back when, I proceeded to jot down what I remembered. My family deserves a bundle of thanks for their unwavering support and assistance as I was formulating this book.

To Mary Denise and Richard for their generous gift of a computer and printer. Without these electronic geniuses this book would have never got off the ground. Thanks for the many hours of editing and formatting, and when I was on the verge of giving up, telling me, "Mom, you must finish it."

To Karen and Gary for the countless number of exhausting hours they spent in editing, correcting, and scanning what I had written. I must have really frustrated their efforts, as I was continually adding, taking away, or changing portions of the script. Finally I had to be admonished . . . no more changes!

To Joan, for being just a step away trouble-shooter whenever I hit a computer snag in the process of transcribing this book.

To all my family for their encouragement to write down what I know about their roots and about my growing up years. The assistance they gave me, especially with their computer skills, has been invaluable. Because of their help, I got promoted from Computer Dummy to one step above, and my book went to the press.

Thanks for the interest of my friends, especially those with a link to the good old days. Many of them and I walked the same Creechville hills and have much in common. I think this book will bring back vivid memories of the cotton patch, home-spun fun, and "the days back when . . ."

Mary Betik Trojacek

BEYOND ELLIS ISLAND

CONTENTS

PREFACE	1
CHAPTER I	
1901 VOYAGE TO AMERICA – BETIK	21
CHAPTER II	
1902 VOYAGE TO AMERICA – MARUSAK	38
CHAPTER III	
JOE AND FRANCES BETIK, MY MOM AND DAD	68
CHAPTER IV	
LIFE ON THE FARM IN THE 1930s	88
CHAPTER V	
ALL ABOUT VILLAGE CREEK SCHOOL	153
CHAPTER VI	
PRAISE THE LORD	168
CHAPTER VII	
AN END TO SHARECROPPING	176
CHAPTER VIII	
THE TROJACEK FAMILY	203
CHAPTER IX	
THE 1940S...OUR HOMEPLACE	231

CHAPTER X
THE FOUR SEASONS OF THE YEAR –
COUNTRY STYLE   261

CHAPTER XI
HIGH SCHOOL   1943 – 1947   313

CHAPTER XII
CONCLUSION   325

Mary Betik Trojacek

PREFACE

A century ago when my grandparents came to America, Ellis Island in New York Harbor was a magic word to the immigrants. They associated Ellis Island with immigration, even though many came through other ports. When  they got off the ship and walked America's soil, their lives took on a different meaning. They looked at the moon and the stars and saw no limits to their dreams. All they had to

CZECHOSLOVAKIA   The little villages of Březuvky, Doubrovy, Provodov and Želichovice were located close to Zlin. Bechyne was near Tabor

do was give of themselves and work. Thus, the title of this book: ***Beyond Ellis Island.***

My destiny began to form more than one hundred

years ago when cultural, political, or religious circumstances in Europe influenced a mass emigration to America. The people came from Ireland, Italy, England, Germany, Russia, Czechoslovakia, and other countries. At that time Czechoslovakia comprised three provinces: Bohemia, Moravia, and Slovakia. It was part of a vast empire ruled by the powerful Austro-Hungarian Monarchy: The Hapsburg family. This Austrian family dynasty had complete and uninterrupted control over Czechoslovakia from 1526 to 1918. The conditions imposed on the Czechs were harsh and there was little hope of ever getting out of bondage. The Czechs had lost their wealth and independence and were deprived of national status or a voice in government. Being reduced to slavery, they had limited access to land ownership and were denied the right to hold public office. The official language of the empire was German. In 1848, the Magyars of Hungary and the Czechs revolted against the German-speaking rulers of Austria. After years of conflict and struggle, the Magyars finally won equality with Austria, and in 1867, the dual monarchy of Austria-Hungary was formed. The position of the Hungarians was elevated, but the status of the Czechs did not change; their lives remained in the same rut. Austria imposed a strict military conscript making it mandatory that all boys, beginning at a very early age, serve time in the Austrian army. To escape from the oppression, the bondage, and the conscription, people were looking for a way out. They had heard of America because colonization in the new world had been going on for years. Many saw this as their opportunity to escape. They sold what little possessions they had or just abandoned everything and bought ship fare and sailed to America.

To get to America, they crossed the Atlantic Ocean, and the only way they could do that was to go by ship. The shipping companies were eager to transport as many passengers as possible, often crowding their ships to over-capacity. The rich were put into roomy suites, but the poor were crammed into below deck economy cabins, called steerage, often used for shipping cattle and other animals. Transporting people was lucrative and boarding criteria was not strict. The most important requirement was to pay for

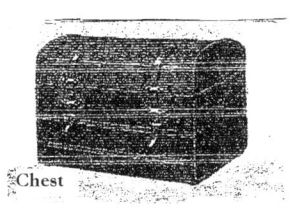
Duffle Bag

Chest

passage. The ships sailed under different flags, departed from different ports, and on board were people from different countries who were leaving their homeland for different reasons, but all were leaving with the same desire; to improve their way of life. As they ventured out into the unknown and the unexpected, many were unaware of the sacrifice and the measure of endurance that would be demanded of them. Dysentery, typhoid fever, and other illnesses were rampant on board the unsanitary and crowded ships.  Treatment was limited or unavailable, and as a result, many passengers did not survive the four to six week journey at sea. It is said that at Ellis Island, New York, there are rooms full of silent witnesses to their fate: piles of unclaimed trunks, boots, coats, other items, and remnants of unfulfilled dreams. The survivors, though tired and weary, had reason to rejoice, they were at the doorstep of America. Most of the ships navigated into New York Harbor and went through The Narrows, known as the "Gateway to the New World." The ships passed by Liberty Island on their way to the

Immigration Center, and the passengers on board could view the most magnificent lady of the times, the Lady of Liberty . . . what a sight to behold! She was the reigning symbol of hope and freedom. The Immigration Center on Ellis Island was the principal immigration station for the people coming from Europe. There were other ports of entry along the Atlantic coast. My grandparents entered America at Galveston, Texas.

Beyond Ellis Island

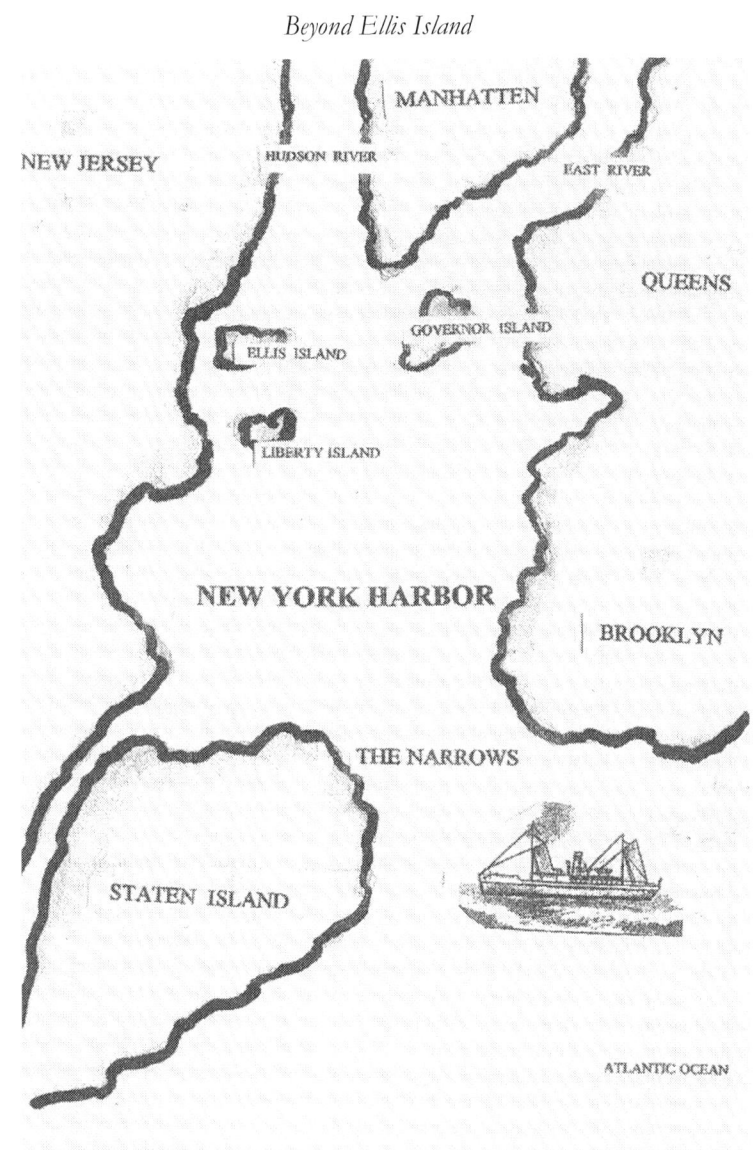

"THE GATEWAY TO THE NEW WORLD"

When the immigrants got off the ship they were screened, checked, and documented. All the new arrivals from Europe had to go through this process after they arrived (Many were screened before they boarded the ship.) Those with infectious diseases, mental illness, ill-repute, or known criminals were denied entry. I don't know what happened to those unfortunate people who didn't pass inspection, because many had spent their last dime on ship fare, and had nowhere else to go. Many were sent back to their native country. The Czech immigrants began arriving in Texas as early as the 1850's when Texas was a new state in the union. The numbers were few and the politicians were eager to populate this vast frontier. In order to attract more settlers, the state offered land grants to those who were willing to come and live here and work the land. Many of the new settlers took advantage of this offer and with this free land were instant landowners. As a result, they sent letters to friends and relatives still in the old country. These letters contained glorious reports of freedom, prosperity, and the opportunity to own land, describing this new country with unbelievable phrases such as, "In America, the streets are paved with gold," or "we have so much in America, we see dogs dragging *klobase* sausage across the yard," or other exaggerated words of enticement like, "fried squab, practically fly into your mouth." In the old country, fried squab, (young pigeon), was a craved delicacy. It was hard to ignore these fascinating and appealing reports and their minds began to work on the belief that there was hope for a different way of life. They were also paying attention to the advertisements placed by shipping companies eager to expand their growing business of transporting immigrants. Speculators in America needing factory or farm workers, sent agents to Europe to "sell" America. The countries abroad did not restrict emigration because poor harvests, famines, and political unrest had strained countries' resources.

Immigration offices were closed during the Civil War, but when the ban was lifted, the European immigrants came in record numbers, especially from the 1880's to the early 1900's. The influx was causing concerns in government. A head tax of $2.00 was imposed on all new arrivals to help relieve the expense of administration and the extra paper work involved. By 1901, when my grandparents came to America, land grants in Texas were no longer available and new settlers were faced with bewildering and overwhelming hardships. Many were penniless because they had spent all they had just to get to America. For survival, they had to rely on each other; therefore, they settled in groups and formed communities. They were also dependent on the earlier seasoned immigrants who, by this time, had established some status and were landowners because of the land grants. The earlier arrivals had learned enough English to get by, knew their way around, and were acquainted with the law of the land. Having sponsored some of the newcomers, they served as "go-between" interpreting and witnessing legal procedures and documents for court records. Many of the sponsors, owners of hundreds of acres of land, divided their acquired land into small farms, built a little house on each one and let the newcomers sharecrop for them until they could buy their own. The landowner made money without having to work the land himself. Now and then, unhappy tales were told how some of the new immigrants were victimized and swindled in business transactions. A bond existed amongst all the Czechs simply because they identified with each other; however, there was not too much social mingling between the seasoned ones and the newcomers. I thought perhaps it was because the new felt beholden to the old, or the old had exploited the new.

The steady flow of immigrants coming to America, continued for several years and on some days as many as 5,000 or more, were screened in one day. A headline in a turn of the century article read "The immigrants just keep coming and coming." After the check-point, most of the people went on to further destinations. The earliest ones by oxen drawn wagons, on a stage coach, or on horseback; the later ones had the choice transportation advantage of going by train. They went with anxiety and apprehension to unfamiliar ground and uncertain expectations, but they had an ever-enduring drive to make a successful change in their lives.

The Ennis, Texas area was attracting many of the new arrivals from Czechoslovakia. My grandparents were among the immigrants from Czechoslovakia who comprised nearly seventy-five percent of the immigrants to Ellis County at the turn of the century. The rich and fertile black lands of North Central Texas beckoned to their skills of tilling the land, cultivating and harvesting crops. Many Czechs by nature were farmers; however, most had learned a trade early in their lives so they would not be dependent on farming alone. The farms in their homeland were so small it was difficult to support a family. To make ends meet, they worked as an apprentice in an established business and learned the arts in boot making, weaving, glass making, and other skills that might be of benefit to them. Many of the women worked as servants in the homes of the upper class. When the new immigrants arrived in Texas, they could not believe their good fortune when they learned they had the opportunity to own land, not just a little plot, but many acres! On top of other skills they already had, they learned to grow cotton successfully, making cotton their main cash crop for decades.

Not all the Czechs who came to Ennis, Texas were interested in farming like my grandparents were. Many thriving businesses were owned and operated by Czechs. Most of them were concentrated in the northern section of town and all the Czechs patronized them because they were able to communicate. This is where they congregated and visited, made deals and transacted business. Here they shopped for groceries, hardware, dry goods, and a hamburger could be had for five cents. The Czechs minded their own business, spoke their own language, and had large families. They were "different" and did not have time to mix with high society. They appeared backward to many people who labeled this north section of town as "The Arkansas Block." Even though they were viewed as backward, they had visions and were workers. One cannot overlook the enormous contribution the Czechs have made towards the growth of Ennis, not only as farmers and business owners, but also in other Czech oriented establishments vital to the family unit. Not many small towns can boast of having the number of grand and spacious halls like those found in Ennis. These fraternal lodges, built by Czechs, on Czech values, served as gathering places for meetings, weddings, dances and other social affairs for members and their families. Later these halls were made available to the entire community. Not many small towns can claim credence to a church and parochial school complex like we have in Ennis. St. John Nepomucene Catholic Church, in all its splendor, is a majestic testimony to the visions and works of the Czechs. As the church bell tolls each day, the pealing sounds fill the air and resonate all around, touching many souls with a quiet peace. The Annual Polka Festival, inspired by Czechs many years ago, attracts thousands of fun-loving visitors each year, putting Ennis, Texas on the map in a unique way. At this festive time, many local folks and visitors from afar, dress in colorful Czech costumes called their *Kroj*. Groups of young people dressed in their *Kroj* often get together to dance the *Beseda*, the national folk dance of Czechoslovakia.

Dance Costumes "Kroj"

They are an attractive and entertaining compliment to Czech celebrations.

The Sokol movement, founded in Czechoslovakia in 1862, promotes physical fitness, group gymnastics and patriotism, and has a strong influence and support in Ennis. The Sokol athletes fine-tune gymnastic skills in a modern athletic center, and their performance qualifies them to enter national and international competitions.

Ennis is represented by many different nationalities, but in my early childhood, as far as I knew, there were only these groups: Moravian (*Moravci*), Bohemian (*Bohumini*),

Mexican *(Meksikani)*, Colored (Černošy), Jewish (Žide), and Americans *(Amerikani)*. This last group included the Irish, English, French, Italian, and so on. All were lumped into this single category called *Amerikani*. I often heard my relatives say, "*Mi sme Moravci*" meaning, "We are Moravians." The Moravians and the Bohemians stuck together when it came to "push and shove," because they were Czech; however as a routine, the Moravians resented being called Bohemian, and likewise the Bohemians let it be known they definitely were not Moravian. Most of the Moravians were Catholic and the Bohemians we knew, belonged to the Brethren Church, sometimes called Free Thinkers. It seemed to me like a cultural rivalry existed, in a subdued way, between the two, each clinging to their distinctive dialects, religion, and culture. After World War II, a blending of the two cultures began, abroad and in America, and in 1993 Moravia and Bohemia were united as one nation and is now known as the Czech Republic. A harmonious relationship has developed and the distinction of whether one is Moravian or Bohemian has been dropped. All are simply called Czech, even though each group respects the identity to their unique history, heritage, and dialect. The language of the Moravians and the

Bohemians is Czech and basically the same, except for a few variations in dialect. For example: the Moravians call their Grandmother, Stařenka, and their Grandfather, Stařiček, while the Bohemians call their grandparents Babička and Dědeček. In our household we spoke Czech with the Moravian dialect, the neighbors spoke Czech with neighbors and the school kids spoke Czech with classmates. When I started school, only then did I begin to learn a second language . . . English. Our teachers spoke only English and our textbooks were written in English only.

Most of the dry goods stores were owned by Jewish families and the Czechs had a good rapport with them. My Mom and the other Czechs shopped in their stores often. I remember visiting in these stores many times and I think I would know Mrs. Burke, Mr. Romick, and the Rothschild brothers even today if I were to meet them on the street. The merchants learned a few pet phrases in Czech, crucial to successful bargaining with a Czech who spoke little or no English. A conversation ensued in Czech, (prompted by the storekeeper), when Mom was trying to decide on a piece of fabric, *"To je zdarma, nic to nestoji"* meaning, "it's cheap, doesn't cost anything." Mom could drive a good bargain too, and would reply, "*Kdyš to ňic nestoji, toš mi to daj*" meaning "If it doesn't cost anything, just give it to me." It seemed the *Amerikani* had the advantage and the upper hand in many situations because they spoke English.

I grew up on a farm in Ellis County in North Central Texas, about nine miles east of Ennis, in an area called Creechville. It was not a village or a town as such, and wasn't even on the map, but it had an identity of its own and everyone knew where it was whether they lived on the south, the north, or west side of Ennis. The ten mile stretch of FM 1181, going east from Ennis toward the Trinity River, was homesteaded only by Czechs. For years, the cotton field landscapes, the frame homes, and the names on mailboxes just didn't change; they were fixed. All the kids who lived in this area around us went to Village Creek Common School District #112, and the 3 to 5 mile radius in any direction from the school was known as Creechville. It was such a stable community. We felt secure in a civilized and trusting world where there were no strangers. No one locked their doors . . . didn't even have a key. The idea of locking doors and putting bars on windows to keep intruders out was unthinkable. That would have been an insult to our neighbor and fellow man. In time of need or bad luck, everyone was a good neighbor.

Examples of the family names fixed on mail boxes that left a lasting impression on the history of Creechville were: Bětik, Bouška, Brožek, Fabera, Galetka, Haškovec, Holy, Janiček, Jarešh, Janoušek, Jurčik, Krajča, Mach, Marušak, Matouš, Patak, Petr, 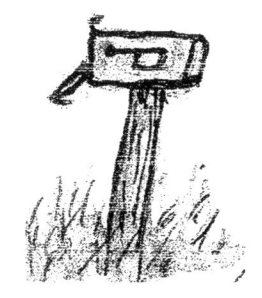 Skřivanek, Slovak, Slovaček, Taraba, Trojaček, Trpak, Vrana, Vrla, Zaidle, Zhanel and Zmolik. (I apologize for any omissions). Any of these fine people living today can relate to Creechville and have many colorful stories of their own to tell. I grew up in this Czech environment among Czech cultures, customs, and traditions; therefore, you will find this writing laced with Czech names, phrases, and expressions.

Illiteracy was rare among the Czechs as they could read and write their language. The old-timers signed their name in proper Czech using the appropriate symbols as seen in the names listed above. For example, my father always wrote Bětik with a little "v" called *haĉek*, above the "e"; Marušaks placed the *haĉek* above the "s", Sedlař placed it above the "r", and Trojačeks placed it above the "c". This denoted a different sound in pronunciation. When the kids started school they stopped using the symbol. This helped them to assimilate into progressive society. And when they ventured out into the business world, their names became Americanized. The Czech dialect slipped away from many of them and the names began to be pronounced with a new linguistic flair. For instance: Betik began to sound more like Betty, and Trojacek began to rhyme with Kojak. As I wrote this story about my life in the '30's and the '40's, I used the *haĉek* only where it was most appropriate, or just left it off.

As I reflect on my life, I cannot help but wonder what my world would be like if my immigrant families had not made the decision to come to America one hundred years ago. The world did not change because of their decision, nor did their decision change world events. A meaning to their life depended on how they viewed the situations around them and how they adjusted to them. They were religious, resilient people with ingenious survival skills who made the best of the most austere situations.

When I wrote about my life on the farm, I did not write about a fairyland. I wrote it the way I saw it and the way I remembered it. Someone else may have seen and interpreted the same situations as entirely different. Many of my entries are fact, some were obtained as a result of my deep interest in reading, some is hearsay and some are merely my assumptions. The details of some escapades may seem unbelievable; some that are sprinkled with humor may bring out a chuckle, while in some parts, it may seem as if it were written with regrets for the way I grew up. There are no regrets. My growing up years were good, wholesome, and happy. I appreciate the many blessings that have come my way as a result of "the way it was." I do not claim authenticity. This documentary evolves from my perceptions, impressions, recollections, and my reflections of what transpired during my formative years. No offense is intended to anyone in this portrayal of my childhood. I value the friendship of everyone who has had such an important part in my life. It is written as chronologically as possible; however, for clarity, references to related incidents may appear more than once. I will make note here that serious genealogists will find a few inconsistencies and discrepancies in data said to be factual. When we consider that most of the information obtained from the immigrants was verbal, and recorded by the clerk the way it sounded, the spelling of names and places may differ from the way it was recorded in a personal journal or the family Bible. The same can be said about dates. Many immigrants lost track of time while at sea and in the days that followed their resettlement. Years later when records were microfilmed, some were already old and may have been damaged, which may have added to some possible variations. To obtain a historical perspective, I have tried to blend in some world events depicting the conditions and circumstances of the times when my grandparents came to America and the years that followed their immigration. These events may or may not have had an impact on their lives or mine. The little entries may give you, the reader, a better understanding of life on the farm before rural America was totally transformed by modern technology, and before the global world was reshaped by a new era of computers, cyberspace, internet, and trips to the moon.

Mary Betik Trojacek

CHAPTER 1
1901 VOYAGE TO AMERICA - -BĚTIK

My paternal great-grandparents, Vaclav and Anna Bětik, were born and lived in Březuvky, Moravia; a little village on the outskirts of Zlin, the nearest town. Vaclav was born September 29, 1837; Anna, August 5, 1838. They married and two sets of twins were born to them. One set died as infants; the surviving twins were my grandfather, Frank Bětik and his sister Anna, born October 5, 1873, when my great grandparents were in their mid-thirties. Even then, friends and acquaintances were already leaving the homeland in search of something better than what they had under the Austrian controlling rule of suppression and oppression.

The Bětiks, my immigrant family, were alert and listening to the reports and the often-repeated phrases of bounty. What they were hearing seemed so wonderful, it was beyond their imagination and comprehension. To be free of bondage, to own land, and have hope for a brighter future seemed like an impossible dream. For years, they had listened to reports and read advertisements about this paradise far away across the ocean. Finally, it began to focus; there was a decision to be made. Like many others before them, their decision was made in near desperation and because they had nothing to lose. It's hard for me to believe that my great grandparents made such a daring move in their advanced years. But in 1901, Vaclav now 64, Anna 63, along with Frank 28, and his twin sister Anna and her husband, Josef Zabojnik and their 3 year old Františka, mustered up the courage to leave everything behind and set their sights on this new world of unbelievable hope and promise. Hardships of unknown dimensions would be dealt with as they were encountered. They packed their necessities in a large trunk, parted with friends and relatives and left their homeland, never to see it again. Czechoslovakia being a landlocked country, made it necessary for them to cross the border to Germany in order to reach a seaport for departure. I assume they traveled by rail because public transportation was already in place. The first railroad in Czechoslovakia opened for public business in 1839. This train took them across Moravia, Bohemia, and Germany, and when they reached Bremen, Germany, they were about 500 miles away from their home near Zlin. On arriving in Bremen, they arranged for passage, boarded the ocean liner named *Norderney,* and sailed to America. Frank had experience in public transportation, and it's been said he worked in the ship's engine room shoveling coal during the three-week voyage,

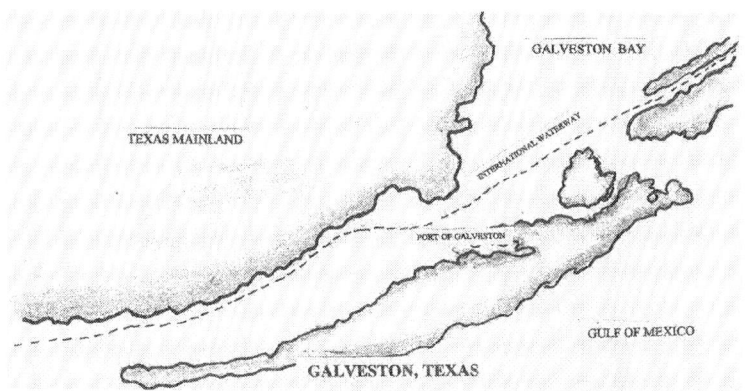

which may have helped to defray the cost of the fare. The *Norderney* and its cargo arrived in Galveston, Texas on June 27, 1901. Here the passengers were screened, checked, and documented. They declared their intent of becoming good and self-sufficient citizens vowing lifelong independence from public and private charities. From Galveston, the immigrants dispersed to various resettlement points primarily in Texas. The intended and final destination of the Betik family was Ennis, Texas, a small community town in its early stages of development, located in North Central Texas. The railroad was already established connecting Houston to Dallas, and went right through Ennis, so I assume they traveled by rail.

Marie Sedlař, my paternal grandmother, was born August 5, 1871 in Doubrovy, Moravia, just a hop and a skip from Březuvky, where my grandfather Frank Bětik lived. Marie Sedlař also made plans to sail to America in 1901. She was Frank's sweetheart in the old country, and perhaps Frank and Marie conspired to make the voyage together, but due to lack of funds (?), lack of sponsorship (?), or lack of her family approval (?); or even perhaps, lack of room on an overcrowded ship, she stayed behind and followed sometime later. It was said she left home on the pretense of visiting relatives, but instead sailed to America. It's not known if she traveled alone or with friends. It's not even known on which day Marie Sedlař arrived in America, or the name of the ship on which she sailed. It is assumed she came through the port of Galveston, but searching through ships' log records have not provided any clues. Perhaps she traveled under an assumed name. Marie was one of eleven children and as far as I know, only one of her siblings, Anna, came to America. She arrived in 1911, ten years later than Marie.

Despite the many hardships and a language barrier, most immigrants made a successful transition. They appreciated their new found freedom, worked hard, and pledged allegiance to their new adopted country. My great-grandmother, Anna Betik, was not a happy camper. She felt deceived by those who had come ahead of her and had sent those glorious reports to friends and relatives still in the old country, reports of such a wonderful life in America. What she encountered was less than wonderful, and she would have gone back to Czechoslovakia in a heartbeat had she had the funds. There were other immigrants who were disillusioned, disappointed and found themselves disadvantaged, but had no money to return to their homeland; however, most felt that in spite of the hardships and civil handicaps, conditions in America were still better than in Czechoslovakia. Above all, they were free. They were not labeled as peasants or serfs and had the opportunity for a better life.

Anna Betik died September 16, 1904, at age 66, three years after she immigrated. Vaclav Betik died November 19, 1911, age 74, ten years after coming to America. Both are buried at St. Joseph Cemetery, Ennis, Texas. Vaclav does not have a grave marker, so the exact location of his grave is not known.

My immigrant family was Catholic, and when they

came to America in 1901, St. Joseph Catholic Church was already recognized as a thriving parish in Ennis, Texas. The services were held in English and the Czechs longed to hear the Gospel in a language they understood. In December of 1901, St. Joseph Church was destroyed by fire, after which the Czechs petitioned the Bishop to allow them to build their own church. Permission was granted. They bought a lot with a house on it on the east side of town, remodeled the house and used it for services while their real church was being built. They named their church *Svaty Jan Nepomucky* (St. John Nepomucene), in honor of a beloved saint in their homeland. When the Bishop provided them with a priest who could speak their

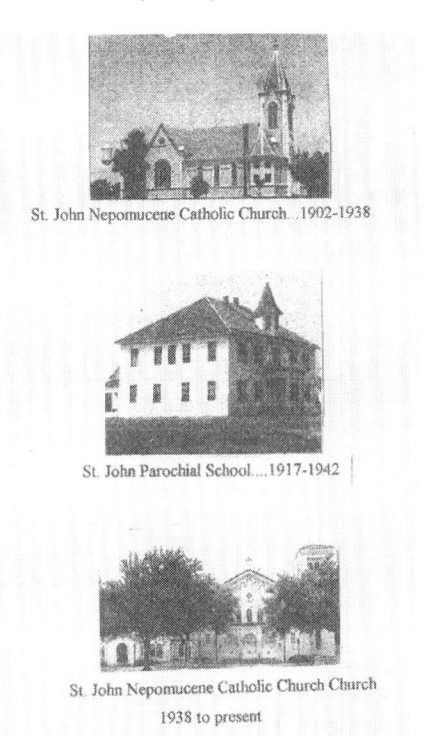

St. John Nepomucene Catholic Church...1902-1938

St. John Parochial School....1917-1942

St. John Nepomucene Catholic Church Church 1938 to present

language, the congregation grew as their religious faith and fervor intensified. My grandparents were there at the inception of St. John Nepomucene Church. The generations that followed them have continued to support it, and in doing so, have witnessed 100 years of growth and expansion of this parish. On May 19, 2002, a Centennial Celebration was held at St. John Nepomucene Catholic Church and focused on the theme, "A Century of Faith." If my grandparents and the other founders were here today, they would see how the humble beginning of their church has blossomed and continued to grow. They would want to tell us that by having a vision supported by faith, love, and endurance, so much can be accomplished. It was as if this message was a whispered inspiration that I pursued the notion of having a monument erected in their honor. This monument was completed in time for the Centennial celebration and now stands by the side of the church as a worthy tribute to those pioneering families. A brief history is inscribed on this 5-foot granite stone, and I hope that everyone who reads it will be touched and inspired by the attributes of those immigrants. Their grandchildren can say with pride, "My grandpa and grandma were there when St. John's Church had its start." The monument was funded with personal contributions from parishioners, relatives and friends. (Nearly one half of the money needed came from the Joe and Frances Betik family.)

After St. Joseph's Church burned in 1901, the English-speaking congregation rebuilt their church and renamed it Holy Redeemer Church. In 1956, the bishop united this English parish with the Czech parish and St. John Nepomucene Catholic Church became multi-cultural. Later Holy Redeemer Church was sold.

Life begins for my grandparents as "Mr. and Mrs. Frank Betik

On arrival to Texas, Marie Sedlař joined the Betik family in Ennis, and Frank and Marie made plans to marry. They were wed July 29, 1902 by Father Wenceslaus Koerner, in the newly established St. John's Church in Ennis, Texas. They settled on a little farm about three miles east of Ennis, belonging to Mr. and Mrs. Žaludek and commenced to sharecrop on this land. Frank and Marie were about thirty years old when their first child, my father, was born. Whenever I go down Creechville Road and pass the Žaludek farm, I picture a little boy named Joe Bětik playing in the yard or in the field while the pioneers Frank and Marie are plowing, planting and harvesting their crops. At the end of the harvest season, they gave 1/4 of the cotton proceeds and 1/3 of the grains to their landowner; some landlords demanded 1/2 of the harvest. That was called sharecropping. About 100 years have passed since my father played there as a little boy. The house is no longer there, but the barn still stands and is in good condition. The farm has changed hands two times and is now owned by friends whom I have known since my school days.

    The dream of every sharecropper was to farm land they could call their own so they would not have to give up any share. My grandparents worked hard. They eked out a living and toiled day by day, but they managed to save. They were keenly aware that opportunities abounded, and if and when one should come up for them, they wanted to be ready to grasp it. Before long, that beautiful day came and they found a farm they wanted to own. It was a perfect farm located on FM 85 about six miles southeast of Ennis. To them America indeed was a land of opportunity! For most Czechs, success was measured by land ownership. All the new immigrants aspired to be part of this class known as land owners and my grandparents were no different. So, when they found this farm and fell in love with it, arrangements were made with Mr. Pechal, the owner to buy it and a deal was made. Included in the price of the farm, or perhaps it was an even trade, six horses were bartered. Land was cheap and could be had for two to four dollars an acre if you had ready cash. Frank and Marie raised their five children on this farm. A century has passed and today it remains in family hands. They would have wished it to be that way. Georgia Patek Ware, who is Frank and Marie's granddaughter, owns the Betik home place on FM 85 and holds the original papers documenting the purchase of the land and other transactions made by Frank and Marie.

Frank Bětik, my grandfather, (Stařícek), as I remember him

I didn't know my grandfather real well because he was ill so much. I remember him as a good and kind man who loved his family and enjoyed their company when they came to visit. During these visits they usually sat around on the back porch. It was breezy there since it faced south, and in the winter time it was warm and sunny and was sheltered from the north wind. My grandfather was a heavy set man of medium height. He had difficulty getting around due to a disabled leg, but he took care of his family and farmed his land and grew cotton and grains as long as he could manage a team of mules and crude farm equipment. I don't know at what point in his life his activity became limited or what had caused his disability. Also, he had lost the sight in one eye when he was quite young. It was said he lost the vision in his eye because of an accident while stoking coals in the locomotives when he worked in the public transportation system in Czechoslovakia. He had many health problems and I never saw him as a well and active man. As he advanced in age, his health declined even more. The vision in his remaining eye deteriorated as his diabetic condition worsened. A stroke followed and he was confined to bed. The early 1940's was a time before the nursing homes came into being, and his daughter, (my Aunt Mary Patek), took care of him in her home. That's the way it

was done then, family taking care of family. He died February 18, 1946 at age 73. I was sixteen years old.

Marie Sedlař Bětik, my grandmother, (*Stařenka*), as I remember her.

My grandmother was a special person. She loved her family, was a good neighbor, and believed in God. Her faith in God made the miracle of birth even more profound each time she helped an infant to be born. With her midwifery skills, she was at my mother's side and assisted in the birth of Lillie, Helen, Mary (that's me), Mildred, Joe, and Bernard.

I remember my grandmother as a slender stately lady who presented the image of an aristocrat, but at the same time, she looked like a true pioneer wife. Her graying hair was brushed back and secured in a bun at the back of her head. Lace and ruffles appealed to her and were seen featured around her collar or down the front of her blouse. The long gathered skirt flowed gently around her ankles and we rarely saw her without an apron. She was challenged by the tedious labor that had to be done on the farm, and took over the many duties when grandfather's handicaps limited him. Although overwhelmed, she learned to harness horses and run a plow, and in spite of it, she always looked like a lady. She worked the fields wearing a long skirt, long sleeve shirt, high-top shoes and a bonnet.

My grandmother possessed much self-learned knowledge and applied it to everyday living. I viewed her as a verbal historian and a philosopher who passed her knowledge and ideas on to family. She believed that when God created the world, He also created laws of nature to keep order in the universe. *Staŕenka* had a firm idea that the processes in nature don't just happen; there are guiding and governing forces that cause them to happen. The sun, the moon and the stars aroused her keen interest and she studied the signs wrought by them. Many seemingly ordinary tasks were done by the signs of the moon whenever possible, tasks such as planting the crops, weaning calves, and setting hens for baby chicks to hatch. There were signs for killing weeds and signs for planting potatoes, signs for transplanting tomato and cabbage plants, and signs for going fishing and making lye soap. Predictions of weather changes were made according to the distinctive ring around the moon, the color of the setting sun, the flash of lightning or clap of thunder in the dead of winter.

My grandmother was a strong woman, but the

elements of nature overcame her; she developed pneumonia and died in the hospital, November 11, 1940. I was eleven years old. Fifteen years later, her great-granddaughter, Joan Elaine Trojacek, was born November 11, 1955. When Joan Elaine was ten years old, her paternal grandfather, Anton J. Trojaček died on her birthday, November 11, 1965. I mention this because it's a notable tribute to the saying, "Life goes on."

My grandparents have been laid to rest in the family plot at St. Joseph's Cemetery in Ennis, Texas. Their pictures are on their tombstones. The family plot is nestled among age-old cedar trees and has been in the Betik family 100 years.

Frank and Marie Bětik Family

Below are a few notes related to Frank and Marie's five children: In the year of 2003, all five children and their spouses are deceased:

1. Joe, their firstborn (my father), April 21, 1903 - March 13, 1968 (one month shy of 65). He married Frances Marušak, February 13, 1904 - January 09, 1991 (one month shy of 87). Ten children were born to them. They will be

introduced later in the course of this writing. Joe and Frances had 49 grandchildren.

2. Louis, second child of Frank and Marie, October 16, 1905 - August 02, 1977 . . . age 71. Uncle Louis married Annie Zapletal and four children were born to them; two of their babies died in infancy. The two children, a son and a daughter that survived were named George and Georgie.

George married Margie (?). She had a little boy named Larry, whom George adopted. Larry Betik lives in Grapevine, Texas. George and Margie had two daughters: Linda and Elizabeth. Linda lives in Lewisville, Texas. Elizabeth died in her early teens. George and Margie have passed away and have been laid to rest at Restland Cemetery, Dallas, Texas.

Georgie Bĕtik Marshel, Uncle Louis and Aunt Annie's only daughter, lives in Grand Prairie, Texas. She has one daughter, Carlotta.

Uncle Louis gave up farming during the war and went to work at a defense plant in Grand Prairie, Texas. Uncle Louis and Aunt Annie are deceased and are buried at Restland Cemetery in Dallas, Texas.

3. Frances, third child of Frank and Marie, November 13, 1906 - November 6, 1983 . . . age 77. Aunt Frances remained single. She spent her lifetime taking care of other people's children. (More about Aunt Frances later in this writing.)

4. Mary, fourth child of Frank and Marie, February 14, 1909 - October 28, 1994 . . . age 85. Aunt Mary married Joe Patek. For a few years after their marriage, they lived on a neighboring farm and then moved to the Betik home place on FM. 85. They had two children: one son named Johnny Joe, and one daughter named Georgia. Johnny Joe, married Rose Krajca, and they had one daughter, Terri. Johnny Joe died August 11, 1988 at the age of 52 (Seven months after the death of his father, Joe Patek). Rose died January 27, 1997- age 59. Georgia, Aunt Mary's and Uncle Joe's only daughter, married Kenneth Ware, and they live on the Betik family farm on FM 85. They have three daughters: Laura, Melissa, and Sharon.

Aunt Mary died at the Betik home place on FM 85 where she had spent her youth. Aunt Mary, Uncle Joe,

Johnny Joe, and Rose are buried at St. Joseph's Cemetery, Ennis, Texas.

    5. Frank, fifth child of Frank and Marie, January 11, 1911 - August 20, 1981 . . . age 70. Uncle Frank married Agnes Jelinek, July 17, 1909 - December 03, 1961 . . . age 52. They had one daughter, Agnes Marie. She married Albert Cox and had two sons, Frankie and Ronnie. After Albert died, Agnes Marie married Ron Lawson. They live in Seagoville, Texas.

    Uncle Frank and Aunt Agnes are buried at St. Joseph's Cemetery, Ennis, Texas, on the same plot as my grandparents - Frank and Marie Bětik, and Aunt Frances. Frank and Marie had seventeen grandchildren. As of this writing I am one of the thirteen that remain living.

Beyond Ellis Island

CHAPTER II
1902 VOYAGE TO AMERICA - -MARUŠAK

Alois and Anna Vaculka Marušak, my maternal grandparents, were born in Holesov, Moravia, a community located north of the town of Zlin. Alois was born June 16, 1867, Anna, February 18, 1869. Later they married and at some point in time moved to Provodov. Provodov was one of many little villages located near and south of Zlin, and was just a stone's throw away from Březuvky and Doubrovy, where the Bětik and Sedlař families lived. Life was not easy for Alois and Anna. Living conditions and the oppressive policies were the same throughout the province since all its' people were subjects of Austria. Realizing that the prospect or hope for a brighter future was never going to improve for them or their children, they read the enticing ads and listened anxiously to the reports of emigrants who had found a new beginning in America and were enjoying freedom, opportunity, and prosperity. And all of this time, their minds and hearts were heavy with indecision, for now they had a family to consider whose precious lives were at risk. If they remained in Czechoslovakia, their future would forever be dim. If they left, they would be subjecting their small children to the harsh reality of resettlement in the incomprehensible New World. After much prayerful and mind searching quandaries, they made the most important decision of their lives and proceeded to make plans to embark on this arduous journey. Needing money for ship fare, they sold the little house they owned for $300.00, packed some necessities in a large trunk, and said their tearful good-byes to family and friends. With their four small children at their side: Anna age 8, Louis age 6, Mary age 4, and Joseph age 1, they left their home in Provodov and made their way to Bremen, Germany, the nearest seaport. Just like the Betiks, they probably traveled by rail. In those days, traveling with four small children, cross-country, and then across the world, must have been an ordeal. When they reached Bremen, they were 500 miles away from the home they left in Provodov. On arrival at the port, they proceeded to make arrangements to sail to America on the ocean vessel named *Koln*.

My Aunt Anna (Kosarek) and Uncle Louis Marusak were youngsters then, but old enough to remember many of their experiences and often related interesting stories. Both recalled one particular incident that took place at customs. There were many people waiting in line to get on board the ship. Aside from ship fare, it was also required that each person, or head of a household, shows $5.00, indicating that they were not traveling penniless to another country. Unknown to the officials, the same $5.00 was passed on from one destitute family to another, allowing several families to get on board using the same $5.00. Another incident that Aunt Anna and Uncle Louis recalled was how distressed their parents were when they saw that they did not have enough money left from the sale of the house to buy ship fare for the entire family of six. They only had enough to pay for five. Would one of the six have to stay behind, and if so, which one? The cost of the ticket was $44.00 per person. Alois' sister, Františka, and her husband, Cyril Zabojnik, loaned them the $44.00 needed to pay for the sixth family member. After all the major hurdles had been overcome, the Alois Marusak family boarded the *Koln* and were on their way to America. The *Koln* was seven stories high and carried 2,300 passengers besides the ship's crew of 1,100.

Františka and Cyril Zabojnik came to America October 11, 1901. The home Alois and Anna left in

Provodov a century ago still stands today and is occupied by one of the "down the line generation."

The three to four-week voyage with four small children must have been very difficult. Coping with unsanitary conditions, diseases, over crowded compartments, and an unsympathetic crew made the journey seem much longer than three weeks. The ship stopped in Baltimore, Maryland, unloaded cargo and picked up other goods, then proceeded through The Narrows and on to New York to the Immigration Center. As they passed by Liberty Island, the immigrants on board were filled with awe at the sight of the Statue of Liberty. Her powerful message emanating to the world reached the depth of every soul gazing in profound wonderment *"Give me your tired, your poor, your huddled masses yearning to breathe free."* The ship docked in New York Harbor where many immigrants got off and then were ferried to Ellis Island. The *Koln* continued on to Galveston with the passengers whose destination was Texas. It arrived there June 16, 1902, on Alois 35th birthday. So now, my grandfather Alois, age 35, and my grandmother Anna, age 33, found themselves in a foreign country surrounded by strangers, and unfamiliar language and customs. Filled with anxiety, they worried about the days ahead, for their journey was not yet finished. The next step was to get to a railroad station where they could board a train that would take them to Ennis, Texas. My Aunt Anna and Uncle Louis often reminisced about those days. Here is another touching story they told. After they arrived in Galveston, they looked for a station where they could obtain transportation to continue their unfinished journey. Not knowing English, it was difficult to obtain directions, but it wasn't long before they got the message, there was not any transportation nearby. My grandparents were not alone in this predicament. There were many people with the same problem in need of a solution. Some were young, some were old, and there were children and babies too. So, what to do now? They resolved to walk. After hours of walking, carrying trunks and children, they got to the place they thought was a train station, but were informed no train stopped there. Night came and the darkness found them by the roadside where some slept and some just waited for daylight. Resuming their walk in the morning, they walked for hours until they reached another station, and to their relief, found it operational. When my grandparents and family finally got on the train they were tired, hungry, $44.00 in debt, and all their worldly possessions were contained in the trunk they carried. The train ride to Ennis probably was the most luxurious experience of the entire venture since they left Provodov.

    I'll make a note here that much has been said, much has been written, and many stories have been told about *Cat Spring*. As far back as the 1850's, the immigrants knew about *Cat Spring*, a little way-station in Austin County about 60 miles west of Houston. It was on the itinerary of many of the immigrants after they got off the ship in Galveston because it was a known dispersal point for many of the new arrivals. First they made their way to Houston on a schooner via the Buffalo Bayou, and then walked from Houston to *Cat Spring*. This 60-mile overland journey lasted about two weeks. Heavy trunks and a few individuals were transported by oxen-drawn wagons. The immigrants had heard so much about *Cat Spring* they expected to find a large town. Instead there were only a few cottages and log cabins in wooded grassland in the middle of nowhere. Here they received some assistance in resettlement. Many of these new immigrants, primarily Czech and German, settled in Austin County and surrounding counties, or wherever they could find land.

Others migrated up the blackland prairie belt to the northern counties. I view the early immigrants like an obelisk, tall, strong and enduring. Their personal will and drive to undertake and continue such a hard and risky journey, and their acceptance of the conditions they faced and endured, makes them heroes in my eyes.

My grandparents did not go via *Cat Spring*. On their itinerary was Ennis, Texas, and they were fortunate that a rail connection had already been established when they were completing the last leg of their journey.

In Ennis they met with their contact person, who took them to the home of a relative, the Zabojnik family, and they stayed there until they found a place with some land so they could grow their own crops. It wasn't long before they moved to a little community called Crisp, located about five miles north of Ennis. At that time, Crisp was a thriving little town and boasted of having a Post Office, a doctor, a cotton gin, a bank, grist mill, and stores. Even a railroad went through Crisp and the town grew on both sides of the tracks. A hundred years has changed many things and today Crisp is a name only. All remnants of the little town are gone and the ghost of Crisp is evident only in the Crisp Cemetery, which has withstood the changing of the times. The cemetery is well cared for and even in this present time, continues to serve the needs of the community. Many tombstones have been there well over 100 years and show marks of erosion caused by the elements of nature. Some inscriptions now are barely legible.

My mother and her brothers, Charles and Frank Marušak, were born in the Crisp community during my grandparents' sharecropping tenure on a farm owned by Mr. Haškovec, who was Alois and Anna's sponsor when they arrived in America. He vouched that they were good people, good workers, and they would not be a drain on the government or charities. My grandparents worked hard to make a living; they scratched, bartered and saved. Their ambition and goal, like that of every Czech immigrant, was to own land. Mr. Haškovec was good to them and after twelve years of sharecropping on his farm and other farms, they were able to buy their own land. In 1914 they purchased a one hundred and thirty-two acre farm in Creechville, a little community about nine miles east of Ennis, on the present FM 1181. Using his carpentry skills he built a two-story house on this farm, and there Alois and Anna raised their family, worked the land, and believed in God. My mother spent her youth on this farm. They were Catholic and their faith was very dear to them. They were there when St. John Nepomucene Church was established in 1902, and like my Bětik grandparents, helped to build it.

Alois Marusak, my grandfather, (Staříček), as I remember him

Alois was a strong willed and ambitious man; he ruled the household and the entire family accepted his decisions. He was a man of many talents: a skilled carpenter, blacksmith, farmer, and inventor. He took care of his family and was a hard worker. Growing cotton was the main source of livelihood for his family and the entire family worked in the fields. Possessing a keen and sharp mind in mechanics, he designed and constructed many of his tools and some of his farm equipment. I especially remember the horse-drawn combine and threshing machine he made to harvest grains like oats, millet, and maize. On the lighter side of inventions, he constructed a mouse trap in the form of a wire cage with a device which permitted the mouse to enter the cage, but could never find its way out. It really worked! (This one must have really impressed me and I think he should have applied for a patent). He did all his farm work barefooted because he was saving his shoes for church. He also did his own blacksmith work and in the process some of the hot coals fell out of the furnace to the ground. It was said he had the toughest feet in town, for he did not even know he was stepping on the hot coals. His strong and robust body stature suggested that he was in good health, but in his aging years he was frequently ill and spent many nights in a straight back chair, wheezing and struggling for a breath of air. When he had these bad episodes, Mom would send one of us girls to spend the night and see to his needs. Health care for my grandparents was almost nonexistent. He lost most of his hair prematurely, and the balding heads of several of his descendants attest that certain genes are passed on; in this case the "bald genes". He was 80 years old when he died on January 23, 1947. I was sixteen years old.

Anna Marusak, my grandmother, (Stařenka), as I remember her

My grandmother was a lady of small stature and so frail it seemed the wind would just blow her away, but she was big at heart, meek, humble, and kind. Most of her time was spent in the cotton patch with Alois. Growing cotton was their cash crop and the whole family effort was put into it. Later, her world became very narrow and confining because of poor vision. It was said she had macular degeneration. Often, I would see her holding her prayer book close to her face to read, but unable to see well, give up in despair. Her dark hair was brushed back, braided, and formed a bun above the nape of her neck. I recall seeing her walk with stooped shoulders and I could tell that those shoulders had carried a heavy load in the past. In spite of her frailties, she lived to age 74. She died January 21, 1943. I was 12 years old. My grandfather Alois, and grandmother Anna, died in the same pale green house where I had spent my early childhood. They have been laid to rest at St. Joseph's Cemetery, Ennis, Texas. Their pictures are on their tombstones. (More about the pale green house later in this writing).

The Family of Alois and Anna Vaculka Marusak

Alois and Anna had seven children: Anna, Louis, Mary, Joseph, Frances (my Mom), Charles and Frank. They are listed here along with their spouses and children.

1. Anna (November 01, 1894 - November 03, 1966, age 72). Aunt Anna married Joseph Kosarek (October 24, 1884 - July 11, 1963 - age 79). They had seven children: Joe, Mary (Reznik, Davis), Agnes (Kozlovsky), Charles, Louis, Leslie, and Frank.

2. Louis (September 29, 1896 - May 16, 1985 ... age 88). Uncle Louis married Mary Spaniel (August 15, 1898 - June 09, 1963 - age 64) Twelve children were born to them: Louis Jr., Mary (Krajca), Johnny, Emil, Ann (Haskovec), Jerry, Emily (Jansky), JoAnn (Mikel, Strunc), Dorothy (Matous), Adell (Pouzar), Henry, and Raymond.

3. Mary (October 17, 1898 - June 28, 1976 ... age 77). Aunt Mary married Frank Salik (April 25, 1898 - December 17, 1892 - age 84). They had four children: Frank, Jerry, Wesley, and Daniel.

4. Joseph (May 18, 1901 - May 26, 1991 ... age 90). Uncle Joe married Agnes Žmolik (January 16, 1907 - May 27,

2003 - age 96). Fourteen children were born to them: Joe, Alice (Sister Agnes Marie), Walter, Agnes (Prachyl), Pauline (Blazek), Helen (Mikel), Leonard, George, Mary Ann (Gagen), Marcy (Krieger), Alex, Kathy, Irene, and David.

5. Frances (February 13, 1904 - January 09, 1991). My Mom married Joe Bětik (April 21, 1903 - March 13, 1968). Ten children were born to them. All ten will be introduced to you as this writing is chronicled.

6. Charles, (Karel in Czech), only lived to about age two. Occasionally, my Mom spoke of her little brother whom she called "*Karlíček*," (an endearing and caressing term for Karel). She was a little older than he and remembered some things pretty well. She said he was a "blue baby", and when they played, sometimes he would cry and turn blue. Mom seemed so sad when she spoke of him. I don't have any other knowledge about "*Karlíček*", and I don't know if there are any records as to where he was buried, etc.

7. Frank (December 17, 1907 - March 06, 1998 . . . age 90). Uncle Frank married Elizabeth Blažek, (we always

called her Aunt Betty) (December 10, 1907 - March 19, 2001 ... Age 93). Fourteen children were born to them: Frankie, Rose Marie (Trojacek), Willie, Georgie (Hejny), Betty (Slovak), Wilma (Kapavik), Lillie (Macalik), Margaret (Martinek), Johnny, Geraldine (Green), Frances (Divin), Elaine (Conner), Elick, and Eugene. Uncle Frank and Aunt Betty celebrated their 70th Wedding Anniversary in 1998.

It makes me think that having a large family is not detrimental to your health; instead, it may be a prescription for longevity. All seven children of Alois and Anna have passed away, as well as their spouses. Aunt Agnes, Uncle Joe's wife, was the last one of that generation to go to her eternal rest. She died May 27, 2003; age 96. The deceased have been laid to rest at St. Joseph's Cemetery, Ennis, Texas.

Alois and Anna had sixty-one grandchildren. (I am one of them). As of December 2003, seventeen of the sixty-one have passed away.

1. Johnny Marusak (Uncle Louis's son). Died January 13, 1927 ... Infant.
2. Frankie Marušak (Uncle Frank's son). Died

December 09, 1941 . . . age 13.
3. Irene Marusak (Uncle Joseph's daughter). Died October 03, 1946 . . . Infant.
4. Frank Salik (Aunt Mary's son). Died October 25, 1971 . . . Age 46.
5. Emily Marušak Jansky (Uncle Louis's daughter). Died February 27, 1963 . . . age 29.
6. Frank Košarek (Aunt Anna's son). Died February 23, 1963 . . . age 48.
7. Wesley Salik (Aunt Mary's son). Died August 8, 1976 . . . age 40.
8. Pauline Marušak Blazek (Uncle Joseph's daughter). Died July 14, 1998 . . . age 63.
9. Leslie Košarek (Aunt Anna's son). Died January 15, 2000 . . . age 70.
10. David Marusak (Uncle Joe's son). Died July 28, 2000 . . . age 49.
11. Louis Marušak (Uncle Louis's son). Died July 30, 2000 . . . age 80.
12. Charlie Košarek (Aunt Anna's son). Died February 5, 2001 . . . age 77.
13. Joe S. Košarek (Aunt Anna's son). Died

November 5, 2001 . . . age 83.
14. Raymond Marušak (Uncle Louis's son). Died November 25, 2001 . . . age 58.
15. Daniel Salik (Aunt Mary's son). Died March 10, 2002 . . . age 60.
16. Ann Marusak Haskovec (Uncle Louis's daughter). Died July 03, 2003, age 73.
17. Emil Marusak (Uncle Louis' son). Died November 02, 2003, age 75.

Five generations have come forth from the humble house of Alois and Anna Marušak, and their Family Tree is laden with branches and leaves representing descendants, totaling more than 654. A Marušak reunion is held every two years, the last weekend of July. It's a fun reunion.

My observations and some items of interest pertaining to the Bětik and/or Marušak families

1. Frank and Marie Bětik, my paternal grandparents, filed for United States citizenship September 11, 1911, and one year later, September 27, 1912, became naturalized US citizens: Certificate #24109. Witnesses on their behalf were

John Gaida and Joe Novy. Frank was called František in the Old Country, but was documented as Frenk (Frank spelled with an "e") on the ship's log and in the county immigration records. (They were in America eleven years before they became citizens.)

2. Alois and Anna Marusak, my maternal grandparents, filed petition for United States citizenship October 1, 1909, and one year later, September 30, 1910, they received their important papers. The names of all the minors living in the household had to be listed on the application and even though my Mom and Uncle Frank were born in America, their names appear on the document too. Mom was listed as Fannie. The Certificate of Citizenship #24107. Witnesses: John P. Krajca and Joe Skrivanek. (They were in America nine years before they became citizens).

3. Most immigrants were eager to obtain United States citizenship, but I wondered why only two certificates were granted in a two year period; noting that the Marušaks received their papers September 30, 1910, #24107, and the Bětiks received their papers September 27, 1912, #24109. In the two years time, only one number separates them.

4. In comparing my father's Family Tree, Frank and

Marie Bětik, to that of my mother's Family Tree, Alois and Anna Marušak, one will find that they christened their children by using the same names: Joe, Louis, Mary, Frank, Frances, and Anna. The Betiks did not have a Charles or an Anna, but if they had a little girl, it's certain she would have been named Anna after my Great-grandmother, Anna Bětik and my grandmother's sister, Anna Sedlař (Vrana, Šulak), and grandfather's twin sister, Anna (Zabojnik.) The names they selected, as well as the names of many other favorite saints, were very common names used in my grandparents' time. Thus, children were named after saints with the belief that having a patron saint at your side on earth was comforting. Having your Patron Saint open the Pearly Gates for you will have profound merits yet to be revealed. It's also worth mentioning that in the Old Country many families referred to the church calendar when naming a newborn. Some named the baby after the saint on whose feast day the infant was born. Also, it was common to give a newborn the same name of a brother or sister who had previously died. (My grandmother, Marie Sedlař, was the second Marie in the family, because a sibling named Marie had died.)

    5. Respect for your elders and those in authority, be

they parents, grandparents, aunts, uncles, teachers or police, was ingrained in younger children. Sass or back talk was not tolerated in homes or schools.

6. My grandparents were proud of the Bětik name and desired very much that it be perpetuated, so that their legacy would live on in the name of Betik. The credit for keeping the Betik name alive and strong must go to my Mom and Dad. If my grandparents were here today, their concerns would be blown away, because they would see the four grandsons (that Mom and Dad gave them); and these four grandsons then gave them fourteen great-grandsons, who then produced for them ten great-great-grandsons and still counting. All Bětik! So the Bětik name lives on, and *Stařenka* and *Staříček* can smile as they look down from above.

7. After the Bětiks came to America, they never saw their homeland or their relatives again. They raised their children to cherish the Moravian dialect, customs and traditions, but did not have the money or the opportunity to go back.

8. The Marušaks had a dream, the same as the Betiks, that some day in their lifetime they could go and visit "the old country" just one time before they died. It remained just that,

a dream, but their dreams resounded in poignant melodies as they sang the many beautiful songs of their heritage, including the national anthem, "*Kde Domov Muj?*" ("Where Is My Home?"); "*Krasna Morava*" ("Beautiful Moravia") and "*Ta Naše Pisnička Česka*" ("Our Czech Song"). The Marušaks were blessed with beautiful singing voices, and just like my Mom, they sang and they sang! My Marušak cousins are still singing even today. They sing in choirs, in groups, and at festivals. Their "singing genes" are a tribute and a testimonial to our heritage. My grandfather sang well too, and he inspired his children with a love for music and their Czech heritage, but what was most touching was the way he expressed his feelings in silence. Many mornings on arising, my grandfather went outside and was seen gazing east in the direction of Czechoslovakia where a part of him had remained.

9. My Mom and Dad each had first cousins named Zabojnik. Grandfather Marušak's sister, Františka, married Cyril Zabojnik. (They loaned them the $44.00 needed for ship fare). Grandfather Bětik's twin sister Anna married Josef Zabojnik. I don't know if these two Zabojnik families were related back in Czechoslovakia. It may be that at that time,

the little villages around Zlin were a lot like Ennis is today. Everyone is related; families are mixed and mixed-up and one will see many of the same faces at all the family reunions.

    10. The trunk that held the meager possessions of the Bětik family on that memorable voyage to America in 1901 belongs to Lillie, (Frank and Marie's oldest granddaughter).

    11. Ernest Tubb, the famous country singer was born in Crisp, Texas (the same community as my Mom.) Perhaps Ernie and Fannie were neighbors?

    12. Galveston, Texas was recovering from the disastrous hurricane of 1900 when the Bětiks came to America. I don't suppose the city appeared very glamorous to them when they got off the ship. Certainly they didn't see any "gold-paved streets." Instead, widespread destruction was still evident, and they must have wondered what they had gotten themselves into. But they were at the point of no return, so on they went undaunted.

    13. 1901, not far from Galveston where the Bětiks disembarked the ocean liner *Norderney*, jubilant crowds in Beaumont, Texas, were celebrating the "Spindletop" oil

strike, the biggest gusher in history. This oil-well alone produced one-half of the nation's oil consumption of that time. However, oil was not my grandparents' concern, quest, or objective. They were in search of black farmland, not "black gold."

14. My grandparents were accustomed to political stress and turmoil in the old country, so when they arrived in Texas, they found their new country facing problems too, though of different nature. In 1901, the year they came to America; President William McKinley was assassinated in Buffalo, New York. Upon his death, Vice-President Theodore Roosevelt became the 26th President of the United States.

15. The country was moving forward and the railroad was recognized as rapid transit. That was the fastest way of getting from one place to another and was greatly patronized. In 1901, the "20th Century Limited" established a new record of railroad speed by going one mile per minute between New York and Chicago. Oxen were being replaced by horses. The world was getting excited about the automobile, and enthusiasts were making great strides in studies, inventions, and testing of the "auto." A segment of the society was so

excited and hopped-up about this new invention they formed an Automobile Club. In a cross-state auto race, three members were arrested for violating the posted speed limit of eight miles per hour. My grandparents were grateful to have a team and a wagon to transport family and supplies and probably made better time and were not even racing.

16. In 1903, one auto maker made headlines because his auto went from New York to San Francisco in just fifty-one days. The Model-A Fords were selling like hot-cakes, and the atmosphere was supercharged with excitement when the Wright brothers flew their "heavier than air" invention at Kitty Hawk, N.C.

buckboard

17. With faith and determination anything is possible. In 1904, Helen Keller, blind and deaf, graduated with honors from Radcliff College. She reminds me of the immigrants who possessed the same attributes, faith and determination.

18. My grandparents were so busy in their efforts to survive; they paid little attention to the Teddy Bear when it made its debut in 1903. On a hunting trip President Theodore Roosevelt refused to kill a bear cub. This

observation inspired the creation of the Teddy Bear which has brought 100 years of cuddles to millions of children, including little Marusaks and little Betiks.

19. About ten years after my grandparents came to America and had their feet well on the ground, the unsinkable *Titanic* sank (1912). If the Norderney or the *Koln* had met the same fate, my destiny would have come to a sinking halt.

20. On June 28, 1914, my grandparents were "doing business as usual," (probably hoeing and cultivating their cotton crop), when World War I broke out in Europe. History has it that two pistol shots signaled the start of World War I. Archduke Francis Ferdinand, a member of the Hapsburg family and heir to the throne of the Austria-Hungarian Empire, was assassinated in Sarajevo. His wife also died in this incident. The Austria-Hungarian Empire, which included Czechoslovakia, was at war again, and all the able-bodied men and boys were conscripted. Once again Czechs in America counted their blessings and good fortune to be away from the havoc of war.

21. The prayers of my grandparents and other Czechs were answered when the Hapsburg Dynasty crumbled in 1918 at the end of World War I and Czechoslovakia finally

gained its independence. However, freedom and jubilation were short-lived, because twenty years later, the Nazis invaded the country and seized its land, its industries and crushed its people. Then came World War II, which lasted from 1941 to 1945. When the war ended, Communist Russia took over and dominated the Czechs for forty-one years; even changed the name of their town Zlin, to Gottwaldov. The Russians made their presence known, and squelched any uprisings or dissension to their rule. Finally, in 1989, the Russian troops were withdrawn, and Czechoslovakia became a democracy. Four years later, the people of the three provinces voted to split and become two separate nations. Bohemia and Moravia united and are known as the Czech Republic. They scratched the name of Gottwaldov and restored the city's former name back to Zlin. Slovakia became known as the Republic of Slovakia.

22. 1920. The U.S. Post Office Department ruled that children may not be sent by parcel post. The Czechs had such strong family values; I don't think this rule would have applied to them.

CERTIFICATE OF NATURALIZATION
Alois (Luis) And Anna (Annie) Marusak

Beyond Ellis Island

Certificate of Naturalization *clarified*

No. 24107   To be given to the person naturalized

The United States of America
Certificate of Naturalization

Petition, Volume <u>1</u>, page <u>10</u>   State Volume <u>2411</u>, page <u>7</u>

Description of holder, Age <u>43</u> years; height <u>5</u> feet <u>7</u> inches; color <u>White</u>; complexion <u>Medium</u>; color of eyes <u>Blue</u>; color of hair <u>Medium</u>; visible distinguishing marks <u>None</u>.

Name, age, and place of residence of wife <u>Annie Marusak, 42 years, resides Crisp, Texas</u>.

Name, age and place of residence of minor children <u>Annie Marusak, 15yrs; Louis Marusak, 14yrs; Mary Marusak, 11yrs; Joseph Marusak, 9yrs; Fannie Marusak, 6yrs; Frank Marusak, 3yrs; all reside in Crisp Texas, Route 2.</u>

<u>State of Texas</u>
<u>County of Ellis</u>   Luis Marusak
      Signature of holder

Be it remembered that at Regular term of the District Court of Ellis Co. Texas held in Waxahachie, Texas on the 26th day of September in the year of our Lord nineteen hundred and ten, Luis Marusak who previous to his naturalization was a subject of Austria at present residing at _____ town of Crisp, Route 2, State of Texas having applied to be admitted a citizen of the United States of America pursuant to law and the

Mary Betik Trojacek

court having found that the petitioner had resided continuously within the United States for at least five years and in this state for one year immediately preceding the date of the hearing of his petition; and that said petitioner intends to reside permanently in the United States had in all respects complied with the law and relations there to and that he was entitled to be so admitted. It was there upon ordered by the said court that he be admitted as a citizen of the United States of America.

In testimony whereof the seal of said court is hereunto affixed on this 30th day of September on the year of our Lord nineteen hundred and ten and of our independence the one hundred and thirty fourth.

Annie Carothers
District Clerk, Ellis Co. Texas

Tribute to the Immigrants

A *Wall of Honor Memorial* stands at Ellis Island, New York, as a tribute to all the early immigrants. These daring, enduring, heroic immigrants, who met untold hardships and suffering in their efforts to reach a common goal to experience freedom and prosperity in this great country. The Czechs must have sung *"Krasna Amerika"* (Beautiful America), with fervency and thanksgiving as they trod America's soil. The *Wall of Honor Memorial* was constructed on Ellis Island through private funding in recognition of the attributes of all the early immigrants, and over the years more than 600,000 names have been inscribed on this wall. Included among them now, are the names of Anna and Vaclav Betik, my great-grandparents, and Frank and Marie Betik, my grandparents. The following names were also entered at this time: Alois and Anna Marusak, my grandparents and their four children born in Czechoslovakia, namely: Anna Marusak Kosarek, Louis Marusak, Mary Marusak Salik, and Joseph Marusak. The inscriptions were made possible through the interest and generosity of their descendants who had the compelling desire to express their sentiments and appreciation to our immigrants for leaving their legacy to those who followed. We are the heirs and beneficiaries of our grandparents' efforts and hard work as they attempted to live out their dreams. All over America, descendants of other immigrants had the same arousal of interest, and over the years had their ancestors acknowledged on the memorial. In 1995, while spaces were still available, the names of our immigrants were inscribed as a special tribute. The cost of inscription per name was one hundred dollars. Lillie Betik Crowley and Helene Betik Barrett were the principal contributors to the Betik memorial.

CHAPTER III
JOE AND FRANCES BĚTIK,
MY MOM AND DAD

Joe Bětik, my father, was born in Ennis, Texas, April 21, 1903; during the time his parents Frank and Marie lived and sharecropped on the Žaludek farm. My father was just a small lad when his parents bought the farm on FM 85. On this farm my father spent his youth. Being the oldest of five children, he had an early introduction to farming; he plowed, planted and harvested. Hunting and fishing were his favorite pastimes, and like his Mom, Marie Bětik, he loved the wonders of nature, and the pleasures and the peace it offered. His idea of a good time was sitting on the river bank baiting trot-lines or strolling through the woods, his shotgun in hand and his dogs at his side. In the spring, he watched his cattle grazing in the green pastures and got excited each time a new calf was born.

Frances Marušak, my mother, was born in Crisp, Texas, February 13, 1904. She was about 10 years old when the family moved to Creechville, and that's where she grew up. She was a pretty maiden and had many friends; they called her Fannie. Fannie was a good sport and could skillfully drive a Model-A Ford; she loved to sing and dance, and to her, picking cotton was a hobby, not a chore. Farming was the only life she had ever known and third grade at Village Creek School was the height of her education. Mom often spoke of the days of her youth and how the young folk created their own social life and good times. For the most part, it was a gathering of friends at a friend's house. It might have been a card or domino game, practicing for a play, or having a barn dance. If the dance was in the house, they moved the furniture around and danced away. Even though communications were not swift in those days, somehow, the word got around about an upcoming event and the Belles and the Gents appeared. Some came toting a guitar, a banjo, a violin, or an accordion. Many romances blossomed at these gatherings, and I suppose that's how Mom and Dad got acquainted and a courtship began. Dad lived on FM 85 about three miles due west as the crow flies from the Marušak home place on FM 1181. Each aspiring young lady who "wannabe a Mrs." had a hope-chest. Mom embroidered

beautiful pillow cases, table scarves, and other items, and added them to her hope chest. I remember when I was a child, we used them for special purposes and on special occasions. Young people often exercised their acting talents and put on plays and presented them on stage at the local hall for public pleasure. The dialogue was in Czech. Even in my childhood, it continued to be popular entertainment. I remember the diligence and dedication of those young hometown actors.

Life begins for Mom and Dad as "Mr. and Mrs. Joe Bětik

My Mom and Dad were married August 11, 1925, at St. John's Catholic Church, Ennis, Texas by Father Francis Kowalski. Dad was 22 and Mom was 21. Before the couple left for church, they knelt down on the floor in front of the parents and received their blessing. The parents made a sign of the cross over them and wished them well. This was a custom in Catholic weddings and I remember doing this too, before my wedding in 1950. Mom was a good cook and a good seamstress and made the wedding cake, designed and sewed her wedding dress and made her veil. The bridal bouquet of white roses was her own creation and she made the roses using crisp organdy. Their wedding party consisted of four couples. The bridesmaids: Frances and Mary Betik (Dad's sisters), Annie Zapletal (later Mrs. Louis Bětik), and Agnes Žmolik (later Mrs. Joseph Marušak). The four groomsmen were: Frank and Joseph Marušak (Mom's brothers), Louis Bětik (Dad's brother) and Thomas Zabojnik (Dad's first cousin). The bridesmaids wore white dresses, style of the 1920's, and each carried a hand-crafted floral bouquet; the groomsmen wore a suit, white shirt and tie. The usual dowry in their day and time was a cow, a pig, a few chickens, and maybe a team of mules and a wagon . . . and always a down-featherbed and a set of down-feather pillows. When Mom reminisced about her wedding, she said all went well on this eventful day, except for one unplanned glitch. A few days before the wedding, they had made oodles of noodles and dried them. The day before the wedding an overzealous cook boiled all the noodles. Since there was no refrigeration, all the noodles spoiled. The guests ate chicken soup with *kapanka* instead of noodles. (*Kapanka* is a loose noodle batter dripped into a pot of hot soup.) Mom said her mother took all the noodles and dumped them behind the barn for the chickens. Today it would be called recycling eggs. The entire celebration took place at the Marusak homeplace: . . the dinner, the supper, and the dance. A platform had been built in the yard and the music was provided by a quickly assembled Czech band of two musicians. One played the accordion and the other a violin. Free beer flowed freely from the keg. A sprig of rosemary tied with a little ribbon was pinned on all the invited guests. They wished the newlyweds happiness and that the marriage be blessed with many children. This was a Czech custom and the herb signified fertility. The guest list included all the relatives, neighbors, former landlords, friends and *Amerikani*, like the sheriff, the banker, the cotton broker, the postman, and those who got a whiff of free food. After their wedding, Mom and Dad wanted to earn some money to start their married life, so they went with a group to Turner Falls, Oklahoma to pick cotton. It was like a picnic to Mom, because she loved to pick cotton. Boarding accommodations were less than desired and the cotton pickers were verbally critical about the conditions. They grumbled in Czech among themselves. When they learned the proprietor spoke Czech too, and understood every word they said, they cut their cotton picking vacation short, packed up and headed for home. On their return to Ennis, the Honeymoon was over. They settled in the Ennis area and commenced to sharecrop, first on the Betik home place on FM 85, where a little homestead stood on the back acres, then a year or so on Juřiček's farm and a year or so on Zabojnik's farm, somewhere around Alma. During the time from 1925 to 1931, their first four children (all girls), were born: Lillie, Helen, Mary, and Mildred. As time passed, six more children were born to them: Joe, Bernard, Wesley, Ella, Evelyn, and Bobby. You will meet all of them as this story is related. As I chronicled this narrative, I added some "newsy" bits of information related to the year when each of Mom and Dad's children were born. Most of it is insignificant, but it helps to broaden one's scope and perspective of those pertinent times. As the children of Joe and Frances Betik are introduced in this narrative, you will meet them by their farm names, in Czech. We always called our Mom and Dad by the endearing term, *"Maminka"* and *"Tatinek" and* never referred to them as "My Old Lady" or "My Old Man." We would not have been a normal family without sibling rivalry, name-calling, taunting, and scuffling. I think there were times when Mom and Dad would like to have exiled all of us.

Joe and Frances Betik Wedding Day, August 12, 1925

Front row: Frances Betik, Joe Betik, Frances Marusak Betik, Joseph Marusak

Rear row: Louis Betik, Annie Zapletal, Thomas Zabojnik, Mary Betik, Frank Marusak, Agnes Žmolik

Lillie, the first of the ten, born December 29, 1926.

Lillie was baptized Ludmila, after St. Ludmila, a saint very dear to the Czechs. Family and friends called her Lillie, Lillian, Ludmila, Litka, Lilka, and Liduša. She responded to all those names, but her farm name was Liduša. By virtue of having been born in 1926, she made an international connection because this is also the birth year of Queen

Elizabeth II of England. Also in 1926, fame came to Gertrude Ederle, a lady from New York, for being the first woman to swim the English Channel. Lillie connected with Hollywood too, because Marilyn Monroe was born this year, and some folks were saddened because Annie Oakley, the sharp shooter, died. In America's high fashion, the flapper dress was the "in-thing," while fashions made out of snake skin were featured in London. Manufacture of automobiles increased steadily, and in 1926, statistics showed that in the United States, the ratio was one auto per six people (very hard for me to believe since Mom and Dad didn't even have one). In England, the ratio was one per 57; in Germany it was one auto per 289; and in Saudi Arabia one auto per 225,000 people. In 1926, Hitler was in jail, but he didn't stop working on his political and frenzied motives and ideas.

Lillie married Lee Crowley on January 18, 1947, (family called him by his baptismal name, Paul). Fourteen children were born to them: Paul Francis, Lillian (Storey), Ronnie, Margaret (Wade), Theresa (Bollech), Mary Ester (Page), Loretta (Caldwell), Edward, Elizabeth (Cabeen), George, Jimmy, Roberta (Wade), Carolyn (Gash), and Richard. Lillie and Paul celebrated their 50th wedding anniversary January 18, 1997. Paul passed away, September 17, 1998. Lillie continues to live in their home on FM 879, Ennis, Texas.

    Growing up on the farm and being the oldest of the children, Lillie learned to cook when she was quite young. After she married and had her family, her cooking skills became refined. She entered cooking and canning competitions at the State Fair of Texas, where she won a multitude of awards. After several years of capturing ribbon after ribbon, the fair officials asked her to stop competing, and instead, be the judge of the hundreds of entries coming in. This generated a lot of interest and many times T.V. and radio personalities looked her up for interviews. She has also been sought out by clubs and organizations to give lectures and demonstrations in food categories. In addition to being a judge and critic of foods, the State Fair Officials invited her to develop a program that would be of interest to the general public. Thus, *Lillie's Country Kitchen had* its start. Each year it has been a daily attraction during the twenty-one-day run of the State Fair. In 2003, Lillie successfully completed her 26th year as host of the event, where she captivated her audience with the simplicity and tastefulness of good old home cooking.

Helen, born November 08, 1928, was found under a bridge ... or, so it was said ...

Helen was baptized Helena Anna. Helen is the namesake of a favorite saint, St. Helen, and Anna, after Grandmother Anna Marusak and Great-grandmother Anna Betik. At the time of her arrival, Lillie was two years old. The year 1928, the year of Helen's birth, is reminiscent of these events: Shirley Temple was born this year; Amelia Earhart was the first woman to make a successful Trans-Atlantic flight; Babe Ruth had just hit his 60th run of the season and in Amsterdam the Vlll Olympic Games were being played. The first television set manufactured in the U.S. was put on the market ($75.00); Henry Ford's new Model-A went on display with an instant back order of 50,000 autos; and in London, a bacteria-killing compound was discovered called Penicillin. Growing up on the farm she was known as Helena or Helenka; in school, Helen; in the business world, Helene. Helene married Bill Barrett and they had two sons; Bill Jr. and Joey. Helene has lived in Dallas, Texas since 1948. Bill Jr. also lives in Dallas. He has two daughters:

Brittany and Ashley. Joey died August 10, 1984.

Mary..... Joe and Frances's third child. That's me, the Depression Kid, born December 25, 1929.

This is the way I perceived it may have been on the day I was born. It's a story put together from what my Mom had told me, and bits of information related to the conditions and circumstances of the times. It has always fascinated me and I think of it as a fairy tale.

Once upon a time on a cold winter night, a feeling of expectation was in the air as the chilling north wind, accompanied with snow, swept across the open country. It was night time and a blanket of snow covered the hills and fields, and obliterated the dirt country road. With the bright snow providing a glimmer of light to see which way to go, Daddy bundled up, harnessed the mules to the wagon and hurried to get Staŕenka Betik to come and assist a new baby to come into this world. Her skills in midwifery were well-known to friends and neighbors who frequently called upon her when "it was time." The effects of hard times were evident all around and everyone was struggling to make a living. The nation's economy had crumbled just two months before, and I suppose Daddy was thinking that bringing a new baby into the midst of it all, was like a depression in a depression. Staŕenka got ready quickly, wrapped up and climbed into the cold wagon. The mules followed the tracks in the snow back to the house. In the dim lamp light, Stařenka applied her expertise and delivered her third grand-daughter. This new baby was me, Mary Betik....... another girl! All hopes of me being a boy to carry on the Betik name were smashed. When I arrived into this world void of hope and promise, the only thing that was bright on this Christmas morning, at 5:00 a.m., was the glistening snow that covered the countryside, and the flickering embers in the wood-burning stove in the corner of the room. Although I may have been a disappointment because I was a girl, they all loved me just the same and let me stay. Lillie and Helen were told that Daddy found me in the snow by the roadside where I had fallen off Santa's sleigh. He heard me crying, so he picked me up and carried me home, "... and then she lived happily ever after." I think it's so nice that my birthday is associated with the birthday of Jesus.

Mom was relieved that I was a strong and robust baby, because she was kept busy with Helen, who was sickly and not thriving well. This went on for quite a while. Finally, it was assumed she was allergic to milk. Her diet was adjusted and she improved. When I think of my Mom and Dad coping with a newborn, a sick baby, and a 3-year-old running around in very primitive conditions, my heart goes out to them. These were the depression years, no money, and no conveniences. I close my eyes and picture those cold and rainy winter days. I see clothes and diapers on the clothes' lines, sometimes frozen stiff. There is a mini clothes line in the house too, strung close to the stove pipes by the chimney, drying a few diapers at a time. How could Mom manage without a washer or dryer, or disposable diapers? Without running water, instant hot water, or electricity? I feel that their love and faith in God is what sustained Mom and Dad through many of their trying times.

Things were pretty bad during the depression and the future appeared quite dismal. One scientist predicted that man will reach the moon by the year 2050. His thinking was gauged on the depressing conditions in America during this particular time. The recovery period after the depression, the war years, and the booming economy triggered man's ingenious mind and developed the means for man to walk on the moon almost 100 years before the predicted time.

The year 1929 was a special year, because it not only was the year when I was born, but also the birth year of Grace Kelly, Princess of Monaco; Audrey Hepburn, British actress, as well as that of Martin Luther King, Jr. It was a bad year because the stock market crashed on Thursday, October 24, 1929, and the country went into panic. Historians refer to this day as "Black Thursday." This year too, Wyatt Earp, the legendary incorruptible lawman died, but remained immortal in rerun movies. The average working girl earned a whopping $33.50 for a fifty-hour work week and farmers were selling their cotton for a pittance . . . 03 cents a pound.

My baptismal record reads Marie Františka. Marie after Stařenka Betik; Františka after Mom. In Czech, I was called Mařenka, Marianka or Mařena. These were my farm names. Attaching a "ka" to the end of a name makes it sound sweet, angelic, and endearing. Most of the time I was called Mařena. In school I was called Mary; as a student nurse I answered to Betik, and years later when I worked at the hospital as a Registered Nurse, I was known as "Mrs. T."

On August 5, 1950, I married Jerry Trojacek. We have seven children. Now they have families and homes of their own and our house is roomy and quiet. August 5, 2000, our children and spouses, and our grandchildren hosted a "Golden Wedding" celebration for us. It was beautiful, elegant and down to earth. We called it "The Party of The Century." We have nine grandchildren and eight great-grandchildren.

Mildred, born July 31, 1931 . . . A crow brought Mildred . . . or, so it was said . . .

When Mildred was born, it was to Staŕenka's dismay, that she too was a girl. The fourth girl! I can only imagine what was going through her mind. *The Betik name will surely die out now!*

In 1931 there were so many crows; they were a threat and menace to the farmers. The corn or grain fields, the watermelon patch and gardens were subject to much damage and destruction if invaded by the flocks of crows. Since there were so many of them and their presence were so prevalent, I guess that's why a crow took the rap for bringing Mildred. She was born in Alma. I was a year and a half old. Mildred made her debut into the world the same year as Joanne Woodward, actress, and Barbara Walters, Journalist. She made a sports connection because Willie Mayes and Mickey Mantle, both baseball greats, share her birth year. Mikhail Gorbachev, USSR Leader, gave her an international link because he too was born this same year. The year 1931 was also the year of the ribbon-cutting and opening of the Empire

State Building, the tallest building in the world at this time. Mildred was baptized Mildred Pauline, named after saints, of course, but her farm name was Milada; her school name was Mildred. She also responds to the name Tillie. I don't know how or why she got hung with an off-the-wall name like Tillie, but it clings to her even today. When Mildred was a toddler, she became very ill after she contracted Scarlet Fever and Diphtheria, a bad combination then. It was on this occasion that Dr. Story saw her and quarantined the whole family. Mildred was sent to Stařenka Betik for two weeks.

Mildred married Adolf Trojacek and they have six children: Danny, Janis (Wensowitch), Judy (Rickman), Marcus, Kathy (Rutherford), and Greg. Adolf passed away February 08, 2002.

In 1932 Charles Lindberg's baby was kidnapped, and this tragic incident resulted in the enactment of new laws to deal with kidnappers. This year the canine actor Rin Tin Tin died, but was resurrected and remains immortal in movies for years to come. Also in 1932, a record was made in United States Immigration history. It was said that for the first time emigration exceeded immigration: 35,576 were admitted, 103,295 left the country. One third were deported, but the majority left on their own initiative. After a few years in America and earning enough money, the emigrants returned to their native lands. Some feared losing their assets during the depression and some, even though destitute, left because they were homesick.

I have only a foggy memory of living in Alma. I vaguely remember playing in a pile of picked cotton, boxed-off and temporarily stored on the front porch. We played and romped in it with the neighbor's kids, Vera Stewart and her brothers. About seventy years have passed since those romping days, and when I occasionally meet up with Vera, I think of her and the fun time we had in a pile of soft cotton on a porch somewhere in Alma in the year of 1933. The country was still in the depth of the depression and everyone was feeling the crunch. Money was scarce; the poor got poorer, and hunger existed in many households, but Mom and Dad were good managers and Daddy never had to stand in the "soup line." We ate what was put on the table and if it didn't excite our palate, we ate it just the same. On the farm we had chickens and eggs, cows and milk, an orchard and a big garden. Daddy was a good hunter and fisherman; he brought "it" home and Mom cooked "it." We were a happy bunch and could laugh about most anything and didn't complain about the way it was.

Sometimes Mom talked about the depression years and how difficult it was for everyone when there was no money. Here is one particular incident she mentioned. It was nearing Christmas and Mom and Dad had no money, but they had some chicken fryers they could sell. If they sold them, they could buy some oranges for their children for Christmas. Daddy took the chickens to Corsicana and stayed there all day trying to sell them. At the end of the day, he brought the fryers back home. No one had the money to buy them. In anguished sadness, Mom said that was one Christmas when their children had no Christmas at all . . . not even an orange.

The year 1933 was about the time we moved from Alma to Creechville to Grandfather Marusak's farm, (Dad and Mom, Lillie, Helen, Mildred and I). I was three years old. Grandfather Marusak, now age 66, and Grandmother age 64, were no longer able to work the land, so the farming operation was turned over to my Mom and Dad, and Uncle Joe and Aunt Agnes Marusak. (Uncle Joe was known as Joseph W. Marusak to almost everyone who knew him, but we always called him Uncle Joe). Each family was to sharecrop one-half of the 132 acre farm. Uncle Joe and Aunt Agnes moved in with my grandparents, into the big two-story house that Grandfather had built for his family. The steps that led upstairs fascinated me; that was the only two-story house I had ever been in.

Mary Betik Trojacek

CHAPTER IV
LIFE ON THE FARM IN THE 1930'S

The Pale Green House

There was another house on this 132-acre farm. It was a three-room frame house painted pale green, and was down the road a piece from Uncle Joe's. We moved into this house and called it home for about seven years. This farmstead also had a barn and sheds; a hog house, a chicken house, a washhouse, and an outhouse. Our favorite place for a playhouse was behind the chicken house. We spent many happy hours there in the years 1933 to 1940. Mom and Dad, and Uncle Joe and Aunt Agnes, got along real well. Mom and Aunt Agnes had a really close relationship, and their loving and trusting friendship lasted throughout the years. Their lives were so entwined, because they had so much in common. They shared joys and sorrows; surprises and disappointments, and enjoyed each other's children, friendship, confidence, and companionship.

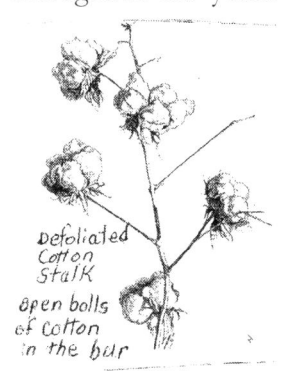

Defoliated Cotton Stalk
open bolls of cotton in the bur

When Mom died January 09, 1991, Aunt Agnes lost her best friend. She felt a deep void and said, "it should have been me, instead." We loved our Aunt Agnes and Uncle Joe, and we spent a lot of time with them and our little cousins. I think we sometimes wondered which household we belonged to. Mom and Dad were godparents for all of Uncle Joe's and Aunt Agnes's children, and they addressed my Mom and Dad as *"Kmotřenka"* and *"Kmochaček,"* a title that demanded a higher level of respect, than just Auntie or Uncle. Since we sharecropped adjoining acreage, it was easy to help each other out when one or the other needed a hand. We often picked cotton side by side. I remember one particular summer. We little cotton pickers really got ticked off at Cousin Walter. He was about five years old; I was about six. He was excused from picking cotton because he had a dermatitis or an allergy on his hands that caused them to be cracked and sore, and the cotton burs just made it worse. So he was allowed to play with the "littler" ones under

The Pale Green House

and around the wagon and the *buda*. *(Buda* described below.) The rest of us kids studied the situation and came to the conclusion that Walter's sores were probably due to the milkweed growing freely in the pasture. We pulled up the milkweed, broke the stems and let the white sap drip into every little scratch we had on our hands. For days we watched our hands for the anticipated results, waiting and hoping to see a change. Nothing happened. We resigned ourselves to the fact that we were put on this earth to pick cotton. That, we understood, but what we couldn't understand was, how come Walter was so blessed!

A *buda* was like a baby bed on two large sturdy wheels. It had a roof, screened-in sides,

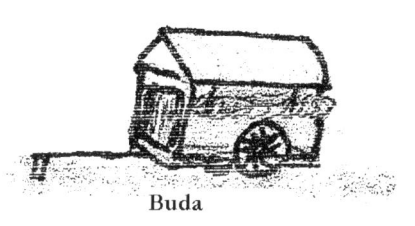

Buda

and a hinged door in the front. The flappers made of duck cloth covered the screened sides and could be rolled up or dropped down, depending from which direction the sun or the wind came. The baby was quite secure from bugs and flies, the sun and the wind. Every farm family had a *buda,* if they had small children. Fire ants were not a worry.

Grandmother Marusak often baby-sat the little ones when the Moms and the Dads went to the fields. She kept the little ones fed and dry. I remember how she cut an apple in half, then carefully scraped out the flesh with a spoon and treated the little ones standing around her, eagerly waiting for their turn. (Applesauce at the height of freshness.) As the kids got bigger and could handle a hoe or a cotton sack, they too, were off to the fields. When Stařenka's health began to fail, one of the older girls, Lillie or Alice, who must have been about eleven or twelve, stayed home to help take care of the smaller children. She also had to wash dishes, sweep the floors, and prepare a meal for the hungry bunch who came in for noon break. Making a go of farming depended on the kindness of Mother Nature and the concerted effort on the part of every family member. Everyone was important. There came a time when the "stay at home baby-sitter/housekeeper/cook" was not expendable. That's when even babies went to the field, so the sitter could lend a hand in hoeing or picking. The *buda,* with few baby care supplies, was hooked up behind the wagon, and we all went to the field family style and everybody had a field day! Sometimes the infant would get restless in the *buda* so Mom would take the baby and nestle it on her cotton sack as she was picking cotton, dragging the sack behind her. Mounds of cotton inside the sack kept the baby from rolling off. The "smart generation" has found other means of coping with a fretful and restless baby, like getting in the car and driving around the block several times until the baby falls asleep.

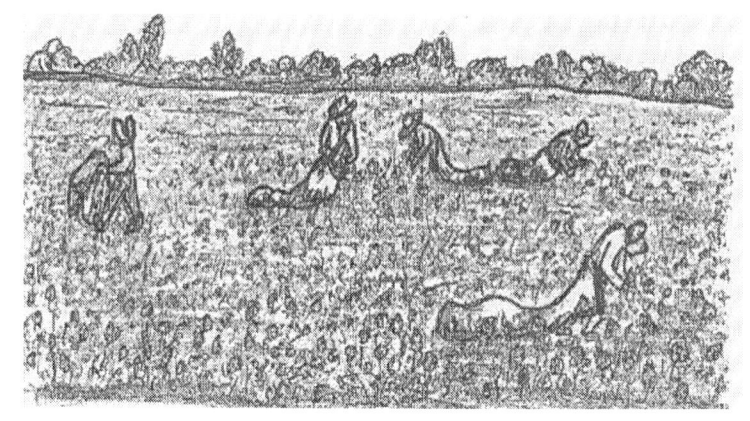

Cotton was the main crop of every farmer living in Ellis County. The bottom-lands along Village Creek were rich and fertile and grew cotton like never seen before, or since. It grew four to five feet tall and was loaded with cotton bolls from top to bottom. If a kid got lost in this cotton patch, all he could see was his bare toes and the ground he stood on, the cotton around him, and the blue sky above. It is interesting to note that during this time Ellis

County had the distinction of producing more cotton than any other county in the state of Texas. Cotton was dubbed as "King Cotton," and continued to hold on to that title through the 1930's. In one year there were 152,601 bales of cotton ginned in Ellis County. All these bales were compressed, and then shipped via railroad to cotton mills or to seaports to be exported. It's often been said, that "King Cotton" and the "Iron Horse" were the two major factors that contributed to the growth of Ennis.

    I was five years old when I began to pick cotton. We truly picked cotton. We picked the white fluff out of the dry, open burs; ever mindful that the bur had to be picked clean and free of any *čičky*, (little fragments of cotton left clinging in the bur.) If we left too many *čičky*, we were scolded. When the gins were equipped to clean out trash more effectively, the farmers went to pulling cotton. The entire opened boll, cotton and bur, was pulled off the stalk and thrown in the sack we were dragging behind us. The length of the sack was six to ten feet long and had a wide strap that fit over the shoulder. Pulling cotton was faster, easier on the fingers, and we no longer had to be concerned about the čičky. When the wagon was full and topped, and containing about 1500 pounds of cotton, it was time to go to the gin. Daddy would let one of us kids go with him each time he made this trip. It was a special day for me when my turn came around. I climbed way on top of the high-framed wagon and sat on the soft cotton next to Daddy; our feet hanging over the front frame. The wagon had a long steel rod stuck vertically down

Going to Gin with Daddy

to the brake control, which could be manned from the top where we sat. A downhill course with a weighted wagon was a tough job for Rubik and Rudik, Daddy's mule team. Brakes had to be applied to keep them from losing it all, including us.

When we arrived at the gin, I ran to the little store for a *Nehi* strawberry soda and some candy. All of us looked forward to a treat from Daddy on our trip to the gin. I remember the little chocolate turtle candies with sprinkles on top and costing only one cent. They were my favorite.

The cotton gin was about four miles from where we lived, and sometimes going to the gin was an all day affair, especially if there were several wagons in line or a breakdown of gin equipment. A wagon-load of 1500 pounds of cotton, ginned out to be about a 500 pound bale of lint, wrapped with wide straps of burlap or hemp and secured with metal bands and made ready for shipping. Daddy was given a sample of the cotton, which was about a 12-by12 inch swath, two inches deep and cut off the side of the bale. Then the

Creechville Cotton Gin

gin operator wrapped the swath of cotton in brown paper (like a big fat jelly roll). Each bale and sample was tagged with the necessary information and the same number. Later Daddy took this sample to the cotton broker who examined it and determined the grade and price to be paid for the bale of cotton. When we got to be about 8 or 9 years old, the gin excursions had to cease, for the cotton sack was a waitin' and the cotton patch was a callin'.

The cotton gins were like the rural schools, conveniently located to accommodate the needs of the farmers. In the 1930's, there were at least 15 cotton gins in Ennis, three within the city limits. The others were scattered over the countryside, Creechville, Telico, Crisp, Bristol, Alma, Bardwell, and several more. At the present time there is only one cotton gin in the Ennis area and it's located in Boyce, a rural community a few miles west of Ennis.

Joe, fifth child of Joe and Frances . . . born in a year of mixed events and emotions.

When my brother Joe was born on June 05, 1934, Stařenka was on hand again to assist with the delivery. Calm, cool, and confident and full of anticipation, she waited for the revelation, boy or girl? I can just imagine the jubilation when she saw a boy! I don't know how she would have handled it if Joe had been a Jo! In June of 1934, the Dionne Quintuplets of Canada were born. Their birth and survival made headline news all over the world. Joe did not even make the local paper "*The Ennis Weekly.*" Joe was baptized Josef František, the namesakes of Daddy and Grandfather Betik. On the farm, he was known as Joška; however, some folks called him Jodie, and a few old timers and some-timers referred to him as Pepik. In school and in the business world he was known simply as Joe. Later Joe married Mildred Lanicek, and they have five children: Alan Joe, Patricia (Zabojnik), Michael, Richard, and Thomas.

The depression lingered on, and people continued to have a hard time making ends meet . . . many losing their farms and other possessions. The rains came, and a heart breaking flood swept through the lowlands and the cotton fields. Our wagon, nearly-full of picked cotton, floated away too, as did Mom and Dad's livelihood and the promise and hope of survival for another year.

The Flood

I remember when this devastating flood occurred. We stayed in the field until dark. Mom and Dad were anxious to have enough cotton on the wagon by nightfall, so he could take it to the gin in the morning. We didn't quite make it. So the wagon was covered and secured with an A-frame type canopy and left in the bottom field overnight; the bale to be finished the next morning. No one was aware of impending weather changes, and before morning the rains came. And it rained, and rained. The creek went out of its banks and overflowed over the bottom-lands transforming the cotton fields into a sea, from the creek to the foot of the sloping hillside. Water flowed rapidly down toward the Trinity River and the current buoyed up the wagon, and floated it downstream like Noah's Ark and parked it against a fence on a neighboring farm. After the water receded, Mom and Dad tried to save the cotton in the wagon, but I don't know how much of it was salvaged. I can only imagine how heavy their hearts must have been seeing their entire crop wiped out. Their tears were tears of despair and hopelessness.

The 1930's continued ...

The year 1934, by virtue of his birth year, Joe can boast of an international link with famous people like: Sophia Loren, Italian actress; Bridgett Bardot, French actress, and Ralph Nader, U.S. Consumer-Advocate. Other figures and events highlighting 1934 were: John Dillinger, the bank robber was caught, put in the cooler and sentenced to 20 years; however, two months after his capture he broke out of jail using a wooden pistol. He claimed he was a good guy, drank very little and hardly ever smoked. The only bad habit he had was robbing banks. The year of 1934 also ended the careers of notorious Bonnie and Clyde, known for robbing banks and businesses. They were stopped cold by the Texas Rangers.

In 1934 a heat-wave in the mid-west killed 206 people in three days. But we felt the heat in Creechville too. The pale green house had no air conditioners or fans and the only reprieve from the heat was a newspaper or a piece of cardboard waved back and forth with hand and wrist motions. Adolf Hitler was out of jail and gaining political power in Germany. The tyranny intensified and many people in Europe were frightened, insecure, and afraid to venture out of their homes. Czechs in America counted their blessings and good fortune, but their hearts and prayers were with friends and relatives they left behind in the homeland. In 1934 Social Security was about to be born. It was just a few months from being enacted into law.

The bottom-lands along Village Creek were good not only for growing cotton, but a natural habitat for pecan trees. As Daddy plowed and cultivated his corn and cotton, he was careful not to damage the volunteer pecan saplings, for he planned to experiment with grafting. Always ready for a challenge, he budded the saplings with paper-shell pecan tree grafts and was so pleased with his high percentage of takes. However, he never realized a harvest from those trees because Mom and Dad moved from this farm before the trees were bearing. Over the years Uncle Frank and Aunt

Betty Marusak derived lots of pleasure from those trees. Some of the trees are still producing today. We lived on Grandfather's farm for about seven years, and during this time, we shared many experiences and good times with our cousins. There was Joe, Alice, Walter, Agnes, Pauline, Helen, and Leonard the baby. Combine the little Marusaks with the little Betiks: Lillie, Helen, Mildred, Joe, Bernard the baby, and me, we could choose sides or form teams. We made up many games, but we had many old favorites too, like kick the can and hide and seek. Stubbed toes were seen frequently because none of the kids wore shoes. Hide and seek was more fun at night. It was a challenge to find everyone on a dark or a moonlit night, but even those in the most secretive hiding places, were quickly discovered when chickens were making funny noises in the chicken house, crackling sounds were heard when a branch broke off a Chinaberry tree and someone fell out, or the dogs with wagging tails were by a tree waiting for a friendly pat on the head. Shooting marbles was a good pastime for boys, but girls could shoot as good as the boys. It was simple to dig out four holes, forming a big "7" (seven), anywhere in the yard and shoot the marbles with our thumb from one hole to another. Every kid used his own strategy with their favorite shooter marble and we played "for keeps." Most of the boys went to school with marbles in their pockets. Hopscotch was boring for the boys, but the girls could hop around on one foot and bend down repeatedly to pick up the scotch and be entertained. Usually a colorful or unique piece of glass from an old broken dish was used for the throw and it was always cheap and easy to come by. We had fun playing Jacks, creating a variety of maneuvers as we bounced the ball and quickly made a grab for a certain number of jacks. The kitchen table, the floor, or the work table in the classroom always made a good play arena. The jacks were made of metal, and if we failed to pick one up off the floor and Daddy found it with his bare foot, he was not hopping with joy. We played games such as Cops and Robbers, Dodge Ball, Drop the Handkerchief, Tsingy-Lingy and many others. City kids thought it was a real adventure to visit on the farm. Farm activity, such as picking blackberries, swimming in the stock pond, craw fishing, gathering eggs, or milking cows fascinated them. They were even good sports when they played "Blind Man's Bluff." One at a time they were led away from the group, then barefooted and blindfolded, were led into a fresh cow paddy. Cruel? Yes, but what a memory!

    The Pale Green House was far from being energy-efficient. Daylight peeked through the cracks around the door and some of the windows. Lillie, Helen, Mildred, and I slept in the north-most room. This room was very cold in the winter, as we had only one wood burning heater in the whole house, and that was in Mom and Dad's bedroom-family room. Often Daddy would go ahead of us and warm up a spot in the icy bed. Then, at our bedtime, we ran into the frigid room; our teeth chattering and our exhaled breath forming little clouds of "smoke." Quickly we hopped into bed, and buried ourselves under the big, thick, fluffy featherbed we called peřina. We moved our feet and legs briskly back and forth to generate more heat, and then we snuggled up close together and were "snug as a bug in a rug" all night. Mom was very generous with the feathers when she made our featherbed. The bed appeared at least a foot higher when it was made up. During a snowstorm, our bed covers were sprinkled with snow that had drifted in through the cracks. We woke up in bliss, because we associated snow with a special treat . . . snow ice cream! The most pleasant memory I have about a snowfall is making snow ice cream. We'd go out and scoop up the mounds of clean snow and make ice cream several times a day, as long as the snow lasted and there was milk in the big stoneware bowl to make more. More than seventy years have passed now since my first memorable snow ice-cream and each new snowfall brings back a vanilla flavored memory. Whenever I see snow begin to accumulate, snow ice cream is a must.

I remember in the early 1930's many country roads were just dirt roads and almost impassable on rainy days. Creechville road was graveled from town and up to the Village Creek School. We lived a mile beyond the school, so when it rained, no one from down our way went anywhere; no one, except the Postman. He went regularly rain or shine and sometimes on horseback. We called him *Poštak*. He had a good rapport with the farmers and did many favors for them. He relayed messages, notified the doctor, delivered medicine, etc. The *Poštak* helped the farmers in many ways, and they always remembered him at hog-killing time and during the holidays. I think the Postman's hardest day must have been when the Sears & Roebuck and Montgomery Ward catalogues went out. Every household got one. Many families shopped for their needs from the catalogue and paid with money order. If they didn't know how to fill one out, the Postman did it for them. When the catalogue went out of date, it continued to be a product availability list and price guide; some folks viewed it as a dream or wish book; and the kids made a neat paper doll collection as they cut out figures and clothes out of the clothing section. The last use for the catalogue was in the *hajzl* (outhouse.) By the mid 1930's, the country was becoming more mobile, and as the mode of travel improved, so did the country roads. Many folks were getting around in automobiles now. For us too, owning a car had begun to be a necessity and Daddy bought a Model-T Ford. We didn't venture out when it looked like it was going to rain. If we got caught in a rainstorm and the wind blew the water under the hood, the motor got wet and the car just "drowned out." We sat there a couple of hours until the wires were dry. During rainy weather, the increased "auto population" created a muddy mess around the church and it

wasn't long before the dirt street in front of St. John's Church was graveled (about 1938). Afterwards, I remember how easily the cars and the buggies could maneuver around. No more ruts or muddy slosh. The gravel was spread only on the church side of the street from the church grounds to the middle. The other half was the responsibility of property owners across the street from church, so that part remained a dirt street for several more years.

The horse and buggy continued to be a respected form of transportation, even though the autos were gaining popularity. On Sunday morning, we could see several teams with buggies tied to a post or a tree near the church. Going home from church in our Model-T, we usually caught up with the Zhanel family who were riding home in their buggy, and Daddy would stop and give the women folk a ride so they could get a head start with Sunday dinner. Cecilia Zhanel Blazek was quite small then and I don't suppose she

FORD V-8—1932
First low-priced car with V-8 engine

remembers those rides in the Model-T. The Zhanels lived about 7 or 8 miles out of town. We lived about two miles further. Sometimes as we rambled down the road in the Model-T, one could see a big block of ice wrapped in a gunny sack, and tied to our back bumper. We made vanilla ice cream in a hand-turned ice cream maker as soon as we got home.

While the Postman, the mail order catalogues, the graveled roads, and the auto, all contributed to improving the lot of the farmer, the farm to farm salesmen played an important role too. (We called them *Pedlak,* derived from the word peddler.) These guys came by sporadically with a variety of wares. Some came by with fruits and vegetables (like apples or sweet potatoes), flavorings and spices; Mom couldn't bake desserts without *Watkin's Vanilla Extract.* Some salesmen came with pharmaceuticals, and some with "you name it" or "whatcha may call it." The farm to farm salesmen provided the avenue to stress-free shopping. The lady of the house could shop while sitting in her favorite rocking chair on the back porch . . . no parking hassle, no cart to push, no little kids in tow, and no shopping bags. From a display on the porch she could select her needs. The Watkin's man came regularly once a month. He was like a drug store on wheels, and some of the best customers he had were my Mom and Dad. We always had *Watkin's Salve*, called *Kafrova Mast* in Czech, and reached for it if we had stubbed toes, mosquito or chigger bites, minor burns, or any other skin irritations. *Watkin's Liniment for Man and Beast*, soothed sore muscles or an aching back. *Hoboko* was an herbal concoction, but I don't know why it was important. *Trinerovo Vino* kept a person regular. The saving grace in a bottle was called *Lydia Pinkum* and was specially made for the fair gender. Many kids got a daily dose of Cod Liver Oil and they hated every drop of the slick, fishy stuff, (no O.J. chaser), but it was rich in Vitamin A and D, and was recommended for children because it prevented Rickets and tooth decay. No one was concerned about cholesterol because they had never heard of it, but now it's part of the daily vocabulary. One ounce of Cod Liver Oil translates to 85 mg. of Cholesterol. Was there ever a home without *Vick's VapoRub*? No way! Vick's, the treatment of choice for the common cold, the cough, or the sniffles. The ailing and firm *Vick's* believers applied it to the chest (front and back), the forehead, the ears, and stuffed a good plug of it up their nose. Nothing was known to cure a sore throat faster than a generous application of *Vick's VapoRub* to the throat wrapped with a flannel rag and pinned with a safety pin. The flannel wrap-around kept the healing powers of *Vick's* focused and contained. Croupy kids sometimes wore it to school. The scent of *Vick's* always followed the dedicated believers. Antibiotics were medicines of the future. Mercurochrome, commonly known as monkey blood, could be found in most households and was used as a disinfectant in cuts and abrasions. Mercurochrome was applied sparingly because it was more expensive than kerosene. A thick salve called *Nonat*, heated and softened with a flame of a lighted match was applied to "boils" or "risens" to help draw out the core. So, in the days of yesteryear, the farm-to-farm salesmen were anticipated, appreciated, and supported. They were a farmer's friend. Mom and Dad enjoyed these visits with the regular *Pedlak* because he was more like company. It's often been said that if a person has faith in a certain product, usually he is convinced that the cure, healing powers, or a long life, can be attributed to its magical treatment. In 1933, a known chemist, died at age 96. He attributed his longevity to a daily ingestion of one spoonful of *Vaseline Petroleum Jelly*, a product he developed in 1870. The saying, "Believing is 99% of the cure," may be something to ponder.

Daddy gravely ill . . . Lock Jaw.

On rare occasions, we hear of a miracle cure. Such was the case of my father's recovery after he had contracted Lock Jaw (Tetanus). We were living in the pale green house when he had become ill after he had stepped on an old rusty nail while feeding the cattle on a rainy day. He often walked barefooted while doing outside chores especially when it was muddy, so his shoes would last longer. The puncture wound he sustained in the heel of his foot was deep and Daddy suspected it could be a problem. He poured kerosene on it to disinfect it (?), and pounded it with a hammer to make it bleed more so all the unclean stuff could flow out with the blood, then soaked his foot in Epsom salt solution. Despite all these commonly practiced first aid measures, a few days later Daddy began to feel ill. Dr. Story said he had Lock Jaw and admitted him to the hospital. Daddy was getting sicker and sicker and his condition was grave. I remember as we stood at Daddy's bed, I saw Dr. Story standing quietly, his head lowered and he slowly shook his head from side to side.

He had exhausted all his expertise and felt so helpless, but he continued to treat Daddy. Several days later, Daddy began to rally and show signs of improvement. We were overjoyed; Dr. Story was amazed and said he had put Daddy in God's hands. After his recovery, Daddy never walked barefooted outside again.

Country Christmas

Everyone has Christmas memories that are special. The earliest recollections I have are from the years that we spent on Grandfather's farm. Each year we looked forward to Christmas, and for us, the holiday season began on December 5, on the Eve of St. Nicholas feast day. We called him *Svaty Mikulaš*. That night, before we went to bed, each of us set out a dinner plate on the kitchen table and put our name on it. In the morning, we were delighted to find fruit, nuts, and ribbon candy on our plate, and we knew that indeed, St. Nick had come by. This was a dear and traditional custom in the old country and was brought to America by our Grandparents. Legend has it that St. Nicholas was a good and kind man who loved children and gave them gifts during Advent. Being kind to others was his way of honoring the birth of Jesus.

Our Christmas tree was a natural, common red cedar. Daddy knew where to find one in the woods because he would identify prospective trees during his hunting excursions. When he brought it home, we thought it was a perfect Christmas tree worthy of our finest decorations and deserved a place in the center of the room. We strung garlands made of popcorn and chain links made with strips of colored pages from an old Sears Roebuck catalogue stuck together with flour and water paste. The few fragile glass ornaments we had, got fewer each time one was dropped. And to make it look like it had just snowed, we put puffs of cotton on the branches and under the tree and overlaid it with a few glistening icicles. For lights we had clip-on candles that were lighted only when Mom or Dad were present. The scent of the cedar mixed with the fruity smell of a few apples and oranges hanging off the limbs filled the room with a pleasant fragrance then, and left us with a sweet memory for years to come. We stopped using the clip-on candles after a near disaster when the cotton on the tree caught on fire. The fire was put out before it caused any damage to the house.

In the 1930's, there weren't as many Santa's Helpers as there are today, so it wasn't often that country kids saw a Santa Claus, (*Mikulas*), much less be visited by one at the house. But one year, while we were at Uncle Joe's and Aunt Agnes's house, we had this rare visit from a real Santa Claus. We were having a jolly good time with our cousins, when we heard someone knocking at the door. Outside it was dark and cold; the dogs were barking and raising cane. Farm folks seldom had visitors in the dead of winter, so who could that be knocking at the door? In questioning anxiety, Uncle Joe opened the door and there stood Santa Claus! Uncle Joe invited him to come in, and when Santa walked in, his companion walked in right behind him. He was wearing a red body suit with a long red tail attached to his back. The tail had a mean looking spear at the tip; the horns on top of his head looked pretty sharp and menacing too. In one hand he carried a pitch fork; in the other a chain, which he shook and rattled as he cast side glances at us. Santa and his companion stood at the door while we stayed our distance and kept an anxious eye on Santa's companion and watched every threatening move he made. Then we heard them asking the Moms and Dads if the kids had been good . . . My, what a scramble to get under the bed! For the next few moments, all that could be heard were the shuffling sounds of the pushing and the shoving coming out from under the bed. We always feared the *Bubak* and the *Has-tr-man,* they were the imaginary monsters of our times, but Santa's companion, this one here in our midst, hey . . . he was for real . . . and we feared he had come to get us and take us all to the burning fires of hell, speared on his pitchfork, chained, or stuffed in Santa's empty sack.

Help! Let me out! I have been GOOD!

Christmas Eve was always observed as a day of fast and abstinence. Children were exempt, but Mom and Dad thought a little penance would do us no harm so we complied too. We were not allowed to eat all day, until the first star appeared in the evening. The day was so long and time moved so slow our hunger pains were wrestling with the urge to taste as the aroma of the feast being prepared stifled us as we helped get supper ready. We made repeated trips outside to see if the Evening Star was aglow. Finally, as dusk was approaching, someone espied the long awaited sign in the western sky and the time had come for us to sit down and eat. We all sat around the long kitchen table (the smaller kids sat on a long bench against the wall), said grace and had a big supper. No meat, but always fish. Usually mackerel fish patties, or Whiting fish rolled in cornmeal and fried in lard. We added our own home-canned vegetables, homemade pies and cakes and fresh bread. Even in the dim light of the kerosene lamp in the center of the table, we saw it as a feast to be remembered . . . one of the best dinners of the whole year. On cloudy days, it worried us, "How will Mom know when it's time to eat if we could not see the evening star?" After supper, we hung up our stockings on the front porch. Each one hung their very own long stocking, beige in color, and made of cotton. We wore them to school and to church on very cold days. They came up above the knees, and were held in place with elastic garters.

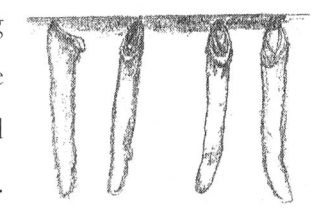

Mary Betik Trojacek

We went to bed full of anticipation. Our night prayers had been said, our featherbed was getting cozy, and our ears were open to hear Shep barking in the night. We listened for the jingling sounds of Santa Claus, but we never knew when he came by. In the morning, we were excited to find an apple, an orange, a banana, rock candy, and a little toy in our stocking. A solid rubber ball, the size of a baseball and costing 5-10¢, lasted all year and brought many hours of fun and play. One Christmas, I also found an 18 inch thin flexible willow stick in my stocking. The little ribbon tied at the end of the switch made it look special, but really didn't change its image or purpose. I don't remember if I was the only one so lucky, or if the other kids got one too.

Country Adventures

As I wrote about my memories of Christmas in the country, images of other experiences and encounters crossed my mind. It's easy to remember situations that happened over and over again, but the rare and unusual ones are the ones that add spice to a memory collection. Now, as I look back and see the idiotic escapades of the days gone by, I wonder how we ever survived childhood. Adventures on the farm were not always under Mom's or Dad's watchful eye; many times we were on our own. How well I remember the days in the early spring, when our cousins (little Marusaks), and we (little Betiks) would hike down to the Village Creek lowlands. The air was clean, cool, and crisp, and the smell of freshly plowed fields made us aware that Spring was just around the corner and the planting season was near. The loose soil felt cool and cushy under our bare feet and crept up between our toes as we walked over the bedded field. Our eyes scanned the creek line and we could see the Redbud trees in full bloom in a rosy shade of pink. They were easy to spot since the other trees had not leafed out yet. Poor little redbud trees, little did they know they were about to be stripped of all their glory! As if our feet were in auto-mode, they led us down the hill, over the levee and across the bottom fields that bordered the creek and on toward those lush Redbuds. When we got to the creek, we tangled with brush and brier, exposed tree roots and vines as we reached for the sweet rose-colored delicacies. We wasted no time as we picked and nibbled the blossoms; then we climbed up the trees and nibbled some more. This was a once a year treat. When we were through, the bare trees looked like the promise of Spring had not even begun to stir. Even though we had this "Redbud Fever," I don't recall that any of us ever got sick.

    Although we were poor, and times were hard during the depression, we were never hungry. Occasionally we ate some unusual cuisine, mostly through curiosity and for the sport of it. Daddy was an expert hunter and frequently brought home rabbit and other wild game. We loved fried rabbit smothered in gravy and experienced the flavors of other wild game such as possum, coon, squirrel, wild goose, and even a crow. Certainly not any of it was detrimental to our health, but the idea of it makes people frown, make facial grimaces, and squirm. There was snow on the ground the day we caught the crows. We could see them at the chicken house eating the corn that Daddy had thrown out to the chickens. Even a blind man could see their jet-black forms against the pure white snow. They were strutting around, greedy and keeping the chickens away. So, Daddy took a wash tub and placed it up side down over the chicken feed and propped up one side with a stick. A string tied to the stick stretched all the way to the house. Now it was time to wait and watch. We thought it was great that Daddy let us participate in his trapping scheme. When the crows had gathered under the tub, we gave the string a good tug. The prop fell out; the tub came down, and we had some trapped crows. Mom made crow soup, adding garlic, onion, seasoning and egg drippings, (a loose noodle batter, called *kapanka*, dripped into a pot of hot soup). There wasn't much meat on the bones, but the taste wasn't bad, after all the crows were corn-fed.

Throughout the years that followed, Daddy's hunting skills got fine-tuned each time a new challenge came up. In the early 1960's, the wolf and coyote numbers were increasing steadily and were getting out of control. They were a threat to the livestock and chickens, and caused the farmers much anxiety and apprehension. So the government set up a Predator Control Program in joint effort with the farmers to help eradicate some of the menacing wolves and coyotes. In this program, a bounty was paid for each pair of predator ears turned in by the farmer. Daddy cooperated with the county government and went to trapping. The venture was an enjoyable sport for him; he got some cash, and in the process helped to eliminate many of the threatening creatures. After he turned the ears in, he hung his earless trophies on the fence posts by the road. In the book, "*History of Telico, Texas,*" on page 287, is a picture of Daddy, his trophies on the fence posts, "Long Tom" leaning against the fence, and Rex his dog-buddy near by. As far back as I can remember, Daddy called his shot gun "Long Tom" and always had a dog-buddy, sometimes buddies. Over the years, I remember Shep, Puntik, Pupik, Tiger, Bobo, Poncho and Rex. The names of others slip my mind.

Adventures and Events of the 1930's continued . . .

Curiosity led Helen and me to dress out some young

sparrows we found still in the nest. Their feathers were full of mites and it was a mess to pluck them. When the critters were clean enough, we fried them and took them to our playhouse behind the chicken house. Imagine this scenario as two preschoolers were preparing to eat their feast of fried sparrows: "Pass me a drumstick, please" . . . "Where is it?" Those were the first and last sparrows served on a dinner table in our playhouse.

Some of the tasks assigned to little kids on the farm could have been catastrophic, but we did what we were told to do and thought nothing about it. As a result, we had some unusual experiences. I don't think Mom and Dad realized the potential dangers in many of the farm activities. Newspapers having limited circulation and other methods of exposure to news not being available to most rural families, Mom and Dad did not know of the many tragedies that occurred elsewhere in the world in everyday family life. We all felt safe and secure and were not keenly aware of the many hazards.

Have you ever felt like you were an acrobat? Now, that's a real experience! One day I was told to go to the barn and throw out all the loose corn shucks from the corn crib for the cows to eat. The outside door to the corn crib was quite high to keep the ears of corn from rolling out. I climbed up into the corn crib and in no time threw out all the shucks. The cows were gathering around, and some were rather rambunctious. As I was coming down out of the barn, one cow hooked her long horn beneath the suspenders of my pants. I was swinging in the air as the cow tried to extricate herself from this sudden surprise that was hanging off her head. I was hollering and waving my arms and legs around, but had no way of getting out of my predicament. Finally, my strap broke and I fell to the ground amongst all those rowdy cows. I was about six years old.

I don't know if Lucifer might have been behind this particular incident, but I remember the day Helen and I got into trouble for eating "forbidden fruit." Mom was saving some especially good peaches for a special purpose, and stored them in the cool cellar. She told us, "Don't eat those peaches." The temptation was great, so Helen and I went down to the cellar just to see what was so special about those peaches. It wasn't long before the cellar door came down with a bang, and suddenly we were enveloped in pitch darkness. Then we heard a thud as Mom had placed a large log on top of the cellar door. As we sat there in this total darkness, we tried to figure out how Mom knew so quickly that we were checking out her peaches. I think Mom handled it like a real diplomat without having said a word.

New challenges fascinated us and were the kind you would not let your own children do. My leg still sports scars from a barbed wire fence accident incurred when I was playing cowboy. (~~Cowboy?~~ Pig boy!) I was standing on top of a board fence of the hog pen, and right there in front of me was Daddy's big boar. He appeared gentle enough, snouting the ground and emitting some friendly grunts as he expected an ear of corn or some other hand-out to drop down in front of him. Instead, I dropped down on top of him. That scared him to death and he took off, but as I straddled him and rode him bareback, I hung on. He took me for a wild ride along the fence line, my leg getting a beating from the barbed wire. (On the farm, we called it "Bob war." We called it like it sounded, long before we mastered the English language.) Bruised and bleeding, I cleaned my leg, poured kerosene over the rips and scratches, smeared them with *Kafrova Mast (Watkin's Salve)*, and then put on some long pants to hide the evidence of my dangerous and foolish feat. We didn't complain much about any misfortunes that befell us; we learned survival skills from some mistakes we made and became wiser because of others. I never went joy riding on a hog again.

Lillie, being the oldest of the children, was usually put in charge of the younger ones. She had more sense, was good at what she did, and smart enough to know when she was losing control. Our Guardian Angels worked very hard helping Lillie and should have earned extra points for working overtime. Some "point-earning" times are described in the following paragraph.

Mom and Dad could have had a heart attack when they saw us scaling the rooftop of the barn trying to catch some pigeons sitting on the peaked roof. We almost caught one too. We never pictured ourselves with a broken neck, arm or leg. Nor did we picture ourselves as lifeless drowning victims when we used Dad's new, freshly painted bee hives, and took them to the deep stock pond and used them for boats. And surely our angels must have been with us with their wings spread out as we jumped out of the hayloft onto a little pile of hay on the ground. What? No broken ankles? The secret lies in having good Guardian Angels. We

Aerobatics

created our own entertainment. Many were original, but some evolved from a natural instinct, like a playhouse. What little girl didn't have a playhouse? Not a structure necessarily, but a little area behind a shed or under a tree marked off as one. Ours was behind the chicken house. We sectioned off rooms using kindling wood, fallen tree branches, logs, or old broomsticks, and swept our floors clean of debris and leaves. In our little kitchen section, we built a little stove out of bricks. Many hours were spent in our playhouse; sometimes we dressed up in grown-up clothes that Aunt Frances had left for us, and we played keeping house and cooking. With a piece of old screen wire, we sifted the dirt and made fine "flour" and "powdered sugar." Using jar tops for pans, a variety of pies and cakes were created. Each one special in its own way. The selection of topping or decor could be maize seeds, tiny rocks, chinaberries, tiny fragments of colored glass, or just let the imagination run free. It was an unlucky day for us when we built a little fire in our stove to bake our goodies and Daddy just happened to see the smoke coming up from behind the chicken house. He caught us playing with fire and we knew punishment was coming. We got a whipping, and never again made a fire in our little brick stove. As if we hadn't learned a lesson from that episode, Daddy caught us yet another time playing with fire not behind the chicken house but this time in a more dangerous place, the barn. Helen, Mildred, and I, still preschoolers, decided we would smoke, and as bad luck would be ours, Daddy just happened to come by and catch us again! When he saw us playing with fire in the barn, he could easily have had a stroke as he envisioned his barn, his Model-T Ford, and all his harvested grain going up in smoke. His shocked reaction was justified and so was the punishment . . . another whipping.

We never played with fire in the barn again.

Mom and Dad rarely spanked us, but playing with fire was serious business, and punishment was in order. Most often, the usual type of punishment for sass or back talk (we didn't sass or backtalk too often) was a twisting pinch of the ear lobe or a *po hlavek* (which means "one over the head"). A *po hlavek* was a swift upsweep stroke-type slap on the back of the head. When we were really, really bad, we got time-out by kneeling on a piece of split kindling wood. Those who snickered or thought it was funny got some of the same. Mom and Dad were very consistent and we could usually anticipate the degree of reprimand or punishment that was our due. The punishment we received did not cause us to be resentful or rebellious, nor did we threaten to run away from home. Where would we go, or what could we do? We knew we were loved, we felt secure and each one of us knew we were an important member of the family, even though there never was a display of hugging, kissing, and other forms of visible expressions of love going on as was seen in some families. Family love and unity came to us in the form of Mom and Dad doing without. Dad fetching a common red cedar tree at Christmastime, or warming up the bed for us on cold winter nights. Love was shown by Mom being a home tutor. She was the buffer when Dad was upset, and she made sure we each had a new Easter dress; Dad shelling pecans at the kitchen table so Mom could make delightful treats for us. We could laugh, Mom could sing, and Dad, with the patience of Job, could sit by the wood-burning heater and disassociate himself from all the background noise we made. He smoked *Mickey Twist* or *Cotton Boll* tobacco in his pipe. His feet propped up and his eyes half closed, he watched the little furls of smoke dissipate into the air. He could relax and stay focused on whatever was on his mind in spite of a bunch of kids around.

Even though Uncle Joe, Aunt Agnes, Mom and Dad worked together really well, there were times when Dad could use more help, so my Uncle Louis and Uncle Frank Betik occasionally came over to help Daddy do some catch-up. After lunch they would lie down on the front porch to rest and smoke. They smoked *Prince Albert Tobacco* and rolled their own. We watched as they held the piece of paper between their thumb and fingers and sprinkled the tobacco on it. There was a certain art to this, and we observed carefully. They always carried their tobacco with them. *Prince Albert* came in a flat thin red container which fit easily into the front overalls pocket. This tin can had the picture of *Prince Albert* on it, and frequently one of the uncles would ask us, "Can you find the number 9 on this can?" Of course we could because the joke was getting old. The number 9 was Prince Albert's ear. I don't know why after all these years I remember Prince Albert and his number 9 ear, but what antique collector today would not be attracted to a Prince Albert can from the 1930's?

Being kids, we followed the examples learned from adults, so a few times we exercised the art of "rolling our own." We gathered dry cotton leaves, took some pages out of the Sears Roebuck catalogue, a few matches, and got out of sight. The best place to go and feel safe from being seen was in the sorghum patch behind the house. There we could sit between the tall rows of cane and do our thing. I didn't get much pleasure in smoking, so I quit early and never smoked again. (Note: The same experience probably applies to my brothers and sisters with all of us kicking the habit way back yonder and to this day remain smoke free.) While we sat there biding our time, we could even have a sweet treat by breaking off a cane stalk, twisting it between the joints, squeezing out the sweet syrupy juice, and being careful not to cut our lips. Or we could strip off the firm outer cover of the cane stalk and chew on its tender inside until all the juice was gone then spit out the remains and take another bite. This is the juice from which molasses is made. One of our neighbors, Mr. Alois Holy, who lived about half a mile away in the Village Creek bottoms, had a mule operated molasses press, and it squeezed out the juice from the sorghum canes. He cooked it slowly in a large vat and it turned to molasses. I remember the time when Daddy brought a wagon-load of cane to him and we watched this process step by step. Now it's a forgotten art. No one makes molasses at home anymore.

Most of our toys were handmade, but we were good at pretending and had a good imagination. Our ages were so close that many similar interests kept us occupied. We had a few dolls during our childhood, but not any of them had real hair or opened and closed their eyes. We knew they existed because we had seen them in the Sears and Roebuck catalogue. I remember this one particular doll we had that was the size of a newborn baby, and she didn't have any hair either. We thought the doll would be so much prettier if she had hair that we could comb and style. The answer to our idea was lying on the back porch step. Old shaggy Shep, sleeping, and unwary, let us do anything we pleased to him. We snipped off his long curls; some black, some white, and with flour and water paste, plastered the curls on the doll's head. The head and face were made of a type of material that blistered when it got wet. The black and white curls stuck together, the head blistered, and the doll looked pitiful. Old Shep? For sure he didn't look like he just stepped out of a dog parlor. Helen, Mildred, and I were preschoolers.

By the mid-thirties communications were improving rapidly, and other means, besides the Pony Express (mail delivered by horse-back), were becoming available. The telegraph, telephone, and radio were well established by now, especially in the cities, but we did not have access to any of them. Our world came alive when Daddy made it possible for us to have an air-wave connection via the radio. The first time I heard *Minnie Pearl* say "H-O-W-D-Y!" was when we were living in the pale green house on Grandfather's farm. Loud-speaking radio was not within our reach yet, but Daddy constructed his own crystal set, and it could pick up the *Grand Ole Opry*. All of us could not listen at the same time, so the earphones were passed around so everyone could hear a piece of something special. It was such a novelty, and it was even nicer when no one else was in the house with whom to have to share the earphones. One day, when I was baby-sitting little Joe (my brother), I had the ear phones on, and I was hearing the sweetest and most beautiful music I had ever heard. Joe was hollering, shaking the baby bed and raising cane, and his tri-cornered wet diaper was hanging below his knees. He was about one year old. I was about five. I made the music stop by moving the little wire that located the station on the little stone and went to tend to impatient Jumping Joe. I changed his diaper and got him quiet. He was happy and I returned to the crystal set thinking I could recapture that beautiful music because my perception was that if I stopped the music on my end of the air wave, it was stopped. I searched and searched as I moved that little wire all over the stone and I never could get it back. I learned something about the radio that day . . . somewhere, out yonder, the band played on!

Speaking of music, just wrap a piece of cellophane around a comb, and hum your favorite tune into it. Your lips will get a thrill and a tickle and the sounds you create are your very own and quite unique . . . Speaking of combs, don't ever twirl your hair on a comb, especially if the hair is long. It never untwirls the same way as it twirls. Speaking of hair, always test a curling iron when removed from hot coals before you curl your hair. You may not have a curl, or hair.

1935

The United States was hit by dust storms. Great clouds of dust hung like a black scourge over many states. Some folks called it the "Dust Bowl." Someone described it as the dust being so thick, even birds were afraid to fly. The dust drifted on into Creechville, and Mom and Dad wondered where all the dust was coming from? They had not fully recovered from the recent flood.

We were living on grandfather's farm in 1935 when Elvis Presley came into this world. He was born in a shack somewhere in Tupelo, Mississippi. I had something in common with the "King" . . . neither one of us were born in a castle. The Hoover Dam Reservoir was completed in 1936 making the reservoir one of the largest man-made bodies of water in the world. Construction of the dam started in 1930, and this project provided work for many who, otherwise, would have been unemployed during the depression. An average of 3,500 people worked on the dam at all times. The entire cost of the project was pegged at $385,000,000.

1936

I was about six years old when I made my first trip to Dallas. Uncle Joe and Aunt Agnes had just bought their new automobile. We all packed in: Uncle Joe, Aunt Agnes, Joe, Alice, Walter; Mom, Dad, Lillie, and I. I don't remember if anyone else went, and if they did, where did they sit? The car was big and looked extravagant and classy. It was black and had a unique chrome design on the rear side of the car, like sometimes seen on a hearse, an "S" leaning forwards. We were so excited on this day, because we were going to the State Fair of Texas. The Texas Centennial celebration was going on at the fair grounds at this same time too. There were so many people there! I had never seen that many people in one day. We followed around as the Moms and Dads viewed the exhibits and the livestock; we visited the aquarium and marveled at the different fish. It was fascinating to see them right in front of our eyes, floating around behind the glass. The highlight was a ride on the Kiddy Car Merry-go-round, the Pony Carousel, and the Ferris

Wheel!

Dallas seemed so big and awesome! The Flying Red Horse on top of the Magnolia Building adorned the Dallas sky line. It looked even more majestic at night with the bright spot lights on it. In 1936, the Magnolia Building was the tallest building west of Washington, D.C., so the Pegasus was in plain view. It is still there today; however, one has to look for it to get a glimpse of it because it is tucked away amongst towering skyscrapers. Though obscured and no longer illuminates the Dallas skyline, it holds a special place in the historic features and fixtures of Dallas. In 1999, a restoration process was started to save the building and Pegasus. The building was being converted to a "turn of the century" hotel. Opening day was set for New Year's Eve, the eve of 2000.

Franklin D. Roosevelt was elected to a second term as President of the US. He won the election in a landslide victory, and people still remembered his speech from 1932 when he said "*The only thing to fear is fear itself.*"

Mary Betik Trojacek

Weddings of the 1930's

    Most of the social activities my family attended were centered around food, beer, music, and dancing. Almost everyone knew the lyrics to the traditional Czech songs, polkas and waltzes. Sing-alongs were common at get-togethers, adding merriment to the occasions. The Czechs had large families, put on big weddings, and were staunch supporters of their heritage in special events and celebrations. I recall some of the weddings we went to in the 1930's. Back then most of the weddings were celebrated at the bride's family home. Preparations for this big event began months in advance. A calf and a pig were fattened, extra chickens were raised, and an ample supply of fruit and vegetables were canned and preserved. Printed or engraved invitations were not sent out; instead, the invitations were extended in person. When the time came to let people know they were invited, the guest list was given to two groomsmen who then went to all the homes of the invited guests and extended a personal invitation. Sometimes the bride and groom themselves went from house to house, and the invited guests felt very honored. Weddings were usually solemnized in church at 9:00 A.M. on a Tuesday. I never understood the logic why it was always a Tuesday, except that it took fewer days away from work in the fields and many of the final preparations could be done over the week-end, especially on Sunday, a designated day of rest from field work. Later, when more country folks got jobs in the city, it became more convenient to have the wedding on a Saturday. Following the ceremony, the wedding party was off to *Maresh* studio downtown to pose for wedding pictures. Meanwhile, the family rushed home to make last minute preparations for the noon meal. The noon meal was called dinner and the evening meal was referred to as supper. In those days it was customary to serve both dinner and supper to the wedding guests. Chicken noodle soup with homemade noodles was a starter at dinner, followed with fried chicken, klobase sausage, potatoes, sauerkraut, vegetables, and a variety of desserts. Fruit-filled pastry called kolačky, apple strudel, as well as pies and cakes were made in family kitchens on wood-burning stoves. I don't remember what the menu was for supper. I think leftovers would have been just fine. Electricity and running water in the rural homes were luxuries of the future. Paper plates and plastic cups were not common household items yet, so dishes, including soup bowls and tableware were borrowed from relatives, friends and neighbors in order to host 100-200 guests. Hired help was rare. All the work was done by family and friends, and the dishes were washed in #3 galvanized wash tubs. The cooks and dish washers, who worked in a steamy hot kitchen all day serving two meals, have my empathy and sympathy however late. It makes me wonder why didn't more parents encourage their kids just to elope?

The usual dowry was a cow, a pig, some chickens, maybe a mule team, a wagon, and always a down-featherbed, *(peřina)* and a set of down-feather pillows . . . this got the marriage off to a warm start!

There were so many people milling around. Most of the guests spent the afternoon outside under trees, socializing, listening to accordion music, singing, and leisurely drinking beer. I also remember the wooden platforms constructed in the front yard of the bride's parents; this was to be the place for dancing. Music was provided by a local Czech band, usually for the price of all the beer they could drink. As time went on into the late 1940's parents wised up and figured out how to best preserve their sanity and prevent their homes from being put to shambles. They began to host the entire event at the hall; scaled down to serving only one meal and serving it on disposable dishes. Today, the catering service is becoming a more attractive and a less worrisome alternative.

Relatives, friends, and neighbors came to these old-time weddings and amongst them usually were a few concerned guests who assessed the skills of the newlyweds. The most commonly voiced concerns were: "Can he provide?" and "Can she cook?" The bride of the millennium has an advantage over the bride of the 1930's. She may not even know how to boil water, but she can put a meal on the table that would be fit for a king. Available to her are so many choices of prepackaged, instant, frozen, cooked-ready to eat, heat and serve, and take-away foods making a delicious meal prepared with very little fret and fuss. And the modern bride gets showered with compliments!

Looking back, I see how so many foods have changed, foods improved, and new ones introduced over the years. As I walk down the aisle of a supermarket, it's good to see oatmeal, cornflakes, saltine crackers, and pork and beans on the shelves just like in the good old days. Those items have not changed; neither has the $1.00 bill. The composition and texture are the same as well as the color and appearance, but when I get to the checkout counter, I find the most significant and invisible difference. The difference is in the number of beans the $1.00 bill bought in the 1930's and the number of beans it can buy today!

Frank and Marie Betik Homeplace on FM 85, as I remember

The memories I have of the Betik home place on FM 85 are special to me because that's where my father grew up. After we moved from the back acres of Grandfather Betik's farm to Alma and then later to Creechville, Mom and Dad would go visit Grandmother and Grandfather Betik. What I note here are just simple recollections of plain and ordinary life on the farm in the 1930's. During these visits Lillie, Helen, and I, and sometimes our little cousin George Betik, explored every nook and cranny on the place while Mom and Dad and my grandparents sat around on the back porch, talked and visited. My grandparents' house on FM 85 stood off the road several hundred feet and tall evergreen trees flanked the wide front porch (The house is still there today, even though it has undergone changes and improvements to fit the needs of a new generation.) A big fenced garden extended toward the road. In this garden grew the usual and the ordinary vegetables, but amongst them one could also find a bounty of what we thought were the exotic and the unusual and the not so ordinary (Like gherkins, Swiss chard, eggplant, artichokes, etc.). Being a curious and creative person, *Stařenka* sometimes prepared special dishes from these not so common vegetables. It didn't impress us too much; we were used to simple foods like potatoes and cabbage. *Stařenka* was a frugal person and didn't like to see food wasted, so she sat at the dinner table with us until our plates were clean. Although ever vigilant, her eyes did rove now and then. We seized this opportunity and quickly slipped some of the stuff into our pockets, or let it accidentally just fall to the floor. *Stařenka* never followed through. I think she pretended poor side vision.

    I remember such insignificant things about the Home place on FM 85 like the woodpile. The split firewood arranged vertically in a tall neat pyramid looked like a big teepee. The Castor Bean bushes around the chicken house hung low to the ground like a canopy and provided cool shade for the chickens. Lillie, Helen, and I found it a neat, cool place too. The chickens didn't seem to mind us, they just moved over a bit, and there was plenty of room for all of us. No one knew then those castor beans were poisonous. And I remember the white moon flowers as big as dinner plates, which graced the fence line by the barn. Every year they came up "volunteers," and the blooms unfolded at night. They presented a pretty picture as they seemed to compete with the moon; however, their fragrance was awful and that was an injustice done to them by Mother Nature. Note: The barn still exists today, and to me, appears no different than it did seventy years ago.

In the front bedroom was a hand-crank phonograph, tall as a chest of drawers. Uncle Frank Betik and his cousin Bob Vrana, both young, single bucks at that time, would lean against it, prop an elbow, and play records and sing along. That's when I picked up the words to the song "*Come And Sit By My Side Little Darlin'.*" Nowadays, this song is rarely or never heard, but whenever I think of it, I get this picture of Uncle Frank and Bob having a jolly good time around the hand-crank phonograph.

The garage was a collector's paradise. Uncle Frank, still single and living at home, collected many things, junk to some folks, treasures to him. A person could find the earliest of license plates, a lot of gizmos and gadgets, failed inventions hanging on the wall or accumulating on shelves or in little piles here and there. Only he knew where everything was. Today they could possibly have some worth. I don't know what happened to them, perhaps there was a huge "Garage Sale?"

The big orchard on FM 85 provided an abundance of fruit. Canning peaches or pears were an all day affair . . . sort of like a Peach-canning Bee, combining work and visitation all at the same time. *Stařenka,* my Mom, Aunt Annie (Uncle Louis' wife), Aunt Mary Patek, and Aunt Frances, got together and exchanged bits of news and gossip, while they pared, cooked, and packed peaches into jars. I recall this new mechanical peach-pear peeler they were using to pare the peaches. Some roving *Pedlak* had talked Uncle Louis into buying it, and he was anxious to see if it really worked as promised. We were fascinated by it and stood around and marveled at this unique invention. I don't know what happened to it . . . perhaps wound up in the garage sale too.

If the orchard failed to produce enough fruit for canning, usually apples, peaches and pears could be bought in quantities from a *Pedlak*. Mom and all my aunts were good at canning and preserving fruits and vegetables and not any of their produce went to waste. Every year the huge Mulberry tree by the garage produced berries profusely. Nothing was thrown away during the depression years and my Mom and aunts thought of ways to put the berries to use. The mulberry jam was not a prize winning product, as the stems turned wiry and the jam did not jell. But what a delightful treat we had fresh off the "tree of plenty." You haven't lived if you had never experienced eating lush, sweet, black mulberries, big as your thumb plucked right off the tree, and savored their sweet goodness After we had our fill, there was no denying where we had been. The berries always left their telltale marks on us, blue mouths, blue feet, blue hands and fingers.

On a little dirt road behind the Creechville Cotton Gin, lived the Lin Wood family. The Betik's had developed a close friendship with this black family and the friendship lasted many years. Lin Wood was a good man and he worked closely with the Betiks at hog killing time, helping in the fields, cutting firewood and other chores. In a way the Betiks understood the plight of the black man, because they themselves had experienced slavery in the old country. They knew what bigotry can do, because the immigrant Czechs often were the butt of jokes, wise cracks, ridicule, and sometimes referred to as *Bohunks* or *Garlic Snappers*. In some instances being known as Czech was considered a handicap in the business world. The Lin Wood family was invited to Aunt Mary and Uncle Joe Patek's wedding, and I remember this day so well, even though I was only five years old. Two meals were served at the bride's home (the Betik's home place FM 85). It was raining cats and dogs that day. Can you imagine serving all the guests dinner and supper on a day like this? After supper, everyone prepared to venture out into the rain to go to the old K.J.T. Hall for the wedding dance. There was mud everywhere and Lin Wood carried the bride, the bridesmaids, and kids to the Model-T cars, so they wouldn't get their dancing shoes muddy. I was a flower girl at this wedding, and cousin George Betik was ring bearer. I was five years old and George was six. For years, Aunt Mary and Uncle Joe Patek called me *Druška*, meaning "flower girl."

    Many, many years later I drove along the road that meandered behind the Creechville gin. (This little road is now known as Gin Road). I was curious to see the landscape changes that had taken place along that country lane where Lin Wood once lived, and I wondered whatever happened to him and his family. Inquiries brought no clues and the folks who might have known have all passed away. The memories of a fine relationship will live on.

And as I remember my grandparents living on FM 85, I also remember their passing. It was customary in those days, after the deceased was embalmed at the funeral home and laid out in the casket, for the body to be brought back to their home and placed in a quiet room where it remained until it was time for the burial. The body could be viewed anytime through a netting draped over the opened casket. The netting was used to present an image of peaceful sleep and also to keep the flies away. To me it was eerie; there was this aura in the room which seemed to fill the air and made you feel you were not alone. The Rosary was said, and friends and relatives took turns and kept vigil all night. Their loved one was never left alone. The practice changed in the 1940's and the body remained at the mortuary until it was time for the burial. All women dressed in black for the funeral. A new widow would continue to wear black for one year after the death of her husband to indicate she was in mourning. I don't remember if an outward display of mourning was required of the man who lost his wife.

All about Aunt Frances

Aunt Frances, Daddy's sister, was born on the Betik home place FM 85. She was quite young when she left the farm and went to the big city (Dallas) in search of her independence. For a young lady to leave home and make a life of her own was considered quite adventurous and gutsy back then. A woman's role in society was to be a stay-at-home-Mom, wife and homemaker, and, of course, work in the fields side by side with her husband. Aunt Frances worked as a governess (nanny), in the homes of wealthy people and took care of their children. Often she talked about the little kids in her charge and the cute things they did. For many years she took care of the children of millionaire H. L. Hunt. We listened attentively when Aunt Frances talked about social graces, table manners, how to meet people, and the proper manner of behavior. Occasionally, she would take one of us to Dallas to spend a day or two with her while she was on the job. She wanted us to see first hand how it was done. She was working for a family in Highland Park, the most exclusive and elite part of Dallas at that time, when she invited me to spend some time with her. I was about eight years old. This particular day some very important guests were visiting; the cook didn't show up, so Aunt Frances took over. Soon she had prepared a very nice breakfast to be served in the fancy dining room. She had cut the grapefruits in half, and asked me to section them (that was the first time I had ever heard of sectioning a grapefruit). She showed me how to do it, so I went on and did as instructed. All done, I proceeded to eat one and had barely got started good when Aunt Frances looked around to see how I was doing. When she saw what I was doing, it almost spun her into orbit. This was the ruination of her day because there were only as many grapefruit halves as there were guests. She quickly composed herself, and removed a section out of each untouched half and placed it in the holes that I had scooped out, and then smoothed it over.

 Aunt Frances liked to bring us fancy clothes, hats, and high-heeled shoes that had been discarded by her Boss Lady. We had such a great time dressing up in them. All decked out in this finery, we paraded to the road and back, several times, and all the time our heads turned, so we could see the neat little imprints the skinny heels made in the dust. The outfits were perfect for playing in our playhouse too. Aunt Frances never married, she just continued to take care of children as long as she was able to. After she retired, she became ill and was in need of assistance in daily living. Georgia Patek Ware (her niece) cared for her in her home until she passed away in 1983.

Hog-killing time and meat preservation

All of the farm folks killed a hog or two every winter and preserved the meat for the days ahead. On slaughter days the neighbors came to help, but even with extra help, it was still quite a chore. Without refrigeration they had to work fast. Usually they chose a day during a cold snap, so the meat would chill out really well and there were no flies around. A lot of hot water was needed during the cleaning process, so a fire was going on under the *kotel* (black iron kettle) a few feet from the action. As the men continued to work with the carcass, we could scarcely wait to cut off a chunk, skewer it on some baling wire and hold it over the flames under the *kotel*. All parts of the hog were utilized; only the squeal was thrown away. Using some of the fresh meat for stew, Mom prepared a nice meal for the helpers.

The hog head was used to make a sausage we called *jitrnice*. Barley was used for filler to reduce the strong meat flavor and the special seasoning made this sausage a Czech version of Cajun Boudin. Not everyone cared for it, but we always liked it and it is still considered a treat today. After the carcass had chilled out overnight, the meat was cut up in small three inches pieces and cooked slowly in the *kotel*. When all the enzymes were rendered out, the meat, submerged in lard, was stored in large ten-gallon stone crocks. The lard prevented air from getting around the meat and kept it from spoiling. Usually we had three or four of these stone crocks full of preserved meat, and supplemented with other meat like chicken, squab, and Dad's game, it usually lasted until the next butchering time. We called this meat *zapečene maso*. Some people called it *oškvarky*. At mealtime, it was simple to go and scoop out enough for a meal and just heat it up in a skillet and presto, the main entrée was on the table. When the meat got low in the skillet, we'd just add more for the other meals. But the best part was fishing out the little chips of meat settled at the bottom of this greasy pan and spreading them over a piece of bread smeared with mustard. Without refrigeration *zapečene maso* was the most common way of preserving meat. Pressure canning sometimes invited spoilage because constant and consistent heat was difficult to maintain on a wood-burning stove. Many farm folks had a smokehouse and smoked their bacon and hams. There was a certain skill required for successfully smoking meat and many farmers did not want to risk spoilage. Most of the cutting, grinding, and sausage making were done at night by the dim light of a flickering kerosene lamp or a lantern. One cold night in 1935, Mom and Dad were working with the meat and had a manual meat grinder set up in the kitchen. The grinder was attached to a chair so one of us kids, assigned to the meat grinding, could manage to turn the handle better. Little Joe was about one year old then, just waddling around, and in his curiosity poked his index finger into the exit hole of the meat grinder. His tiny finger fit perfectly into the little hole in the disc and cutting plate. Assigned to the meat grinding task, I gave the handle a swift turn and amputated his finger at the first joint. Mom and Dad took Joe and the severed finger tip to the hospital hoping it could be reattached, but it could not be done. Every time I see Joe using his hands, I wish I had not turned that handle.

We never butchered beef, only hogs. Cows were raised for milk and for increasing a herd. The ones not needed were sold to supplement the farm income. Hog killing on the farm is mostly an event of the past and most old timers have learned the ways of the "smart generation." When they get a yen for *klobase, ham, or jitrnice* they just buy it at the meat market.

CHAPTER V
ALL ABOUT VILLAGE CREEK SCHOOL

Village Creek Common School District #112 was established around 1894. It was situated on a hill on several acres of open land at the crossroads of Walker Creek Road and FM 1181. In 1898 the student enrollment numbered sixty-one and by 1920 the school had more than 100 pupils, which is quite impressive since there were so many country schools scattered about in the rural areas. The book *"History of Telico, Texas"* features several pictures of the students at Village Creek School. My Uncle Frank Marusak is easily identified and I think I recognize my Mom in one of the pictures too.

1935 I start school . . .

We were living on Grandfather's farm, still sharecropping, when I started school. I was not quite six, but

Mom signed me up anyway. I didn't know any English and my teacher, Mrs. Evarts, didn't know any Czech, but soon I mastered the story about *Henny Penny*, who was upset because her barnyard friends would not help her plant her corn, and *Chicken Little*, who thought the sky was falling. By the end of the school year, I knew English well enough and was promoted to second grade.

Most of my elementary school years were at Village Creek School. The entire school enrollment came from Czech families except for three children. They were *Amerikani* and were from a family even poorer than the other families living in Creechville. Every day for lunch each one carried one dry biscuit. I felt sorry for them and sometimes shared my cold scrambled egg sandwich with them. This was in the mid-thirties and the depression continued. Programs were being set up by President F.D. Roosevelt to help turn the country around by providing jobs for scores of the unemployed. These children's father finally got a job with W.P.A., (Works Progress Administration, which was an expansion of the N.R.A., National Recovery Act). After a few years their lives must have improved because they moved and I didn't hear of them any more.

For many years Village Creek School was 100% Czech except for the teachers. All the kids at Village Creek School were country kids. They lived on a farm, didn't ask for much, and hoeing and picking cotton was their way of life. Absenteeism was high in September and October because kids stayed home and picked cotton. In peak season and good weather, the teachers knew they would have only a few students, so they cooperated with the parents and just suspended classes for a couple of weeks.

In the 1930's, there were many 1-3 room public schools scattered about in the Ennis rural area, and usually, were located about 5 or 6-miles from each other, giving all the country kids an opportunity for some book learning. The schools were identified by geographic name and district number. Most of the kids walked to school, and if they lived on the east side of the railroad tracks they could attend school at Village Creek, Hopewell, Telico, Lone Oak, Crisp, Sand Lake, Alma, Pea Ridge, Mote, or Alsdorf; names of other schools slip my mind. We lived about a mile beyond Village

Creek School and walked two hills up and two hills down each day as we walked to and from school.

The layout of Village Creek School was in the shape of an "L," having three classrooms and a wide hall connecting the front porch and the back porch. The two rooms that adjoined each other had a retractable wall between them which was pulled back on nights of school plays, etc. The trustees built a stage before such events, and then dismantled it after it had served its purpose. Between scenes or acts in the play, some of the local boys, with a banjo, guitar, and violin, played Christmas Carols, Cotton-Eyed Joe, and other numbers. The turnout was always great . . . standing room only. All the parents and families came in support of their children and teachers, but many just considered it a big social event.

Curriculum . . . Grades 1 to 8, were taught at Village Creek School.

There were three classrooms and three teachers. Each classroom had two or three grades, and the one teacher taught all the required subjects for each class. Emphasis was placed on Reading, Writing, Arithmetic, History, and

Geography. Each desk was equipped with an ink well and we dipped our script pens in ink as we wrote our assignments. Fountain pens were available too but leaked often after being filled with ink thus creating a messy paper. Ball point pens were introduced before I finished high school. No bilingual education; even though enrollment was practically 100% Czech. My Mom and Dad's education was limited, but when we stumbled in Spelling, Reading or Arithmetic, Mom came to the rescue; she was our private tutor.

    The wooden floors in the classrooms were oiled to keep the dust down. Periodically, sawdust soaked in scented oil was sprinkled over the floor before it was swept. I think I could recognize that unique smell even today. The school didn't have janitors so the schoolchildren swept the floors and did other housekeeping chores such as cleaning the blackboards, dusting erasers and tidying up. Our library was a shelf which held a Dictionary, a set of *Books of Knowledge*, song books, and a world globe. We had access to library books when every few weeks the teachers exchanged the books at the county library. Each room had a large cloakroom where we hung our coats and put our lunch on a shelf. A big coal-burning furnace provided heat in the winter time. There was one in each classroom. At the end of the school day, a couple of the kids were assigned to bring in two big buckets of coal from the coal bin. Preparations in order to have everything ready to start the fire in the morning. We could always tell which kid had been in the coal bin by the black smudges on their hands and clothes. Behind the coal bin were two big Bois D'Arc trees, and the girls often had a little picnic there. Each one brought a sack of "something" or "anything" and shared. One day someone brought some popcorn balls, and I lost a tooth in this sharing process. The syrup was so stiff I couldn't open my jaws to pry it off my teeth.

    We carried our lunch in a little pail from syrup. *Br'er Rabbit* syrup was purchased in a one-half gallon bucket, and when all the syrup was gone, the little pail with a lid and a handle was a neat way to carry our lunch to school. It was fly-proof and kept the smelly little ants out too. There wasn't much variety in our school lunches. Most of the time we had a scrambled egg sandwich or bits of *zapečene maso* on homemade bread smeared with mustard. (Bologna on store-bought bread was a rarity, a bag of potato chips was a never, and buying *lunchables* would have been a sin.) We wrapped our sandwich in an old newspaper, which was reused several times before it was discarded. And when *Cutrite* wax paper came into being we stepped up in class. Along with Daddy's honey, and Mom's jams, *Br'er Rabbit* syrup was always on hand to use as topping for pancakes or hot bread. It would pleasure me to see *Br'er Rabbit* again.

    At the school our drinking water was outside and came from a long row of fountains situated a top of a long trough. The pump on the well nearby was primed and the water flowed from the fountains at the turn of a spigot. Today this well is the only feature that remains on this site to remind us that a school once existed there. The well is straddled with a windmill pumping water into troughs. Cattle are now roaming over the grounds where hundreds of children had played in the past. Many "old timers" even today, could still draw a map of the old softball field or be able to step it off. Each classroom had many windows so on ordinary days that was our source of light, and when the windows were raised to permit cool breezes, the flies came in as if they had an open invitation. Electricity was already available to the school in 1935, but we used it only on dark and cloudy days. Each room had a light bulb with a long string attached, suspended from the tall ceiling. The string was pulled and just like magic there was light! Electricity was not extended further down to Creechville where we lived, until about 15 years later, but it didn't seem to bother us at home because we had not been used to anything better than a kerosene lamp. Toilets were outside too. A little building down the hill on the south side of the premises was "boys"; on the west side was "girls." They were "multiholers," chemically treated, and had the stamp of approval from the Health Department, (the sanitation requirements of the times). Some of the boys were mean to the girls. The girls' privy provided a quick refuge during scuffles and unfriendly encounters with the boys. Everyone was aware of and respected the invisible no-trespassing line a short distance from the girls' zone. When the boys approached this imaginary line, they put their brakes on. The only way the girls knew how to retaliate to the boys' meanness was to taunt them with silly little rhymes (in Czech) that didn't make any sense, but they rhymed and that's what was chanted. One that comes to my mind went like this. *"Brožek, Brožek, stratil rožek. Petr ho našel, a dostal černy kašel."* Meaning that Brožek lost a horn, (referring to a devil's horn), Petr found it and got whooping cough. The chanting infuriated the boys and made their hair bristle and they dealt the girls a lot of misery. If the girls didn't make it to the security of the girls' house fast enough, the boys pulled them by the hair and kicked them around. Often the score wasn't settled until after school on the way home. Walking down the road there was no refuge, and sometimes the girls landed under the bridge. Christian love between the boys and the girls could have stood a little upgrading.

Recess time, lunch time, class time, began with the sounds of a hand-held, hand-rung school bell. The kids felt privileged when the teacher asked one of them to be the bell ringer.
The teachers who lived in town were among the first in the area to own an automobile. For them it was a necessity. They also used their cars to haul the school kids around if they had no means of getting to certain activities, such as softball and volley ball competitions between schools, 4-H Club exhibits, and other events. Sometimes the truck from the cotton gin was used to shuttle the kids around, (this truck was usually used to haul bales of cotton to shipping points.)

In 1938, Mrs. Hubacek, our teacher, took a carload of kids to see the *Fat Stock Show* in Ft. Worth. It was so far away. I thought we would never get there. We stayed all day. It was the first time I had ever seen cotton candy or a corny-dog on a stick. I was so impressed. I still remember they were so neat, and tasted so good.

Hairdos of the times.

The simplest hairdo of that time was the No-Do, which was a straight cut above the eyeballs and a straight cut below the ear lobes. Pigtails were worn by the girls whose hair was long and straight. A pretty bow was attached at the end of each braid.

Hot Rod Perm

A few of the girls had a beauty shop perm; the hair was rolled on rods and connected to an electric current. This left a frizzy curl, split ends, and telltale blisters on the neckline or scalp from the electric rods. Often the girls looked like they really had got hold of a hot wire. The ultimate hairdo was a copy of the style worn by *Shirley Temple* (child movie star). The hair was rolled in vertical curls all over the head.

When the rollers were removed, the curls were not touched or disturbed with a brush or a comb for fear of losing the effect. If a quick curl was wanted for a special occasion, it could be had with a hot curling iron, manual of course. It had to be heated on hot coals in the stove or the iron could be stuck down the chimney of a lighted kerosene lamp. After a few minutes, it could be tested on a piece of newspaper. If the iron scorched the paper, it was too hot to use on hair. If the iron was applied to hair without first testing, one could hear a sizzle, see smoke, and smell burnt protein . . . and then . . . too bad, so sad! We experimented and improvised with different methods of curling our hair. We used the thin metal strips from coffee cans; the end result was a frizzy curl. If a looser curl was wanted, the hair could be rolled on strips of rags and the curl tied in. If no other equipment, except for *Bobbi pins* were on hand, they worked well for "spit curls." (Spit on your finger tips, wrap a strand of hair around your finger, then secure the curl flat against the scalp with a *Bobbi pin*). Hair spray in a can for longer lasting curls was not available yet, so we made our own. By adding sugar to the hair setting water, it stiffened the curl and the wind didn't blow it apart. We gave up this idea when we discovered that it attracted flies! *Brilliantine* or *Vaseline Hair Tonic* was in every household, and all the boys used it to the max. They put it on so heavy, the slick hair stuck together and little glistening beads of oil could be seen dripping off the ends of their hair.

Most of the girls at Village Creek School belonged to the 4-H Club: Head, Heart, Hands, and Health. The girls learned arts and crafts, sewing, food handling and management, and other homemaking skills. The County Agent planned and scheduled certain projects for us. One such project was to sew a dress. I sewed one with lots of help from my mother. It was made of a blue cotton fabric, with little red hearts printed all over. Heart-shaped pockets trimmed with red rick-rack accented the flared skirt. The girls who had participated in the project went to Waxahachie for a modeling demonstration. (Again, a hat's off to our teachers who provided the transportation.) I didn't win any ribbons, but I did walk across the stage and turned around a couple of times, and that's saying a lot for a bashful and timid girl. I loved this dress and never tired of wearing it. I was about nine or ten years old.

All the country kids went to their nearest public school; however all the Catholic kids went to St. John's

Parochial School for at least part of the time in preparation to receive the Sacraments. Boarding accommodations or transportation had to be privately arranged by the parents. When I was in the second grade, it was thought I had reached the age of reason, so I too could receive the Sacraments. This year, I found myself in Sister Ciprianna's class, learning Catechism, Reading, Writing, Arithmetic, and Czech. I had spoken Czech all my life so it was easy to learn to read and write the language. Built in 1917, this school was a white, two-story frame building. Besides classrooms, this building also served as a residence for the nuns. The classrooms were

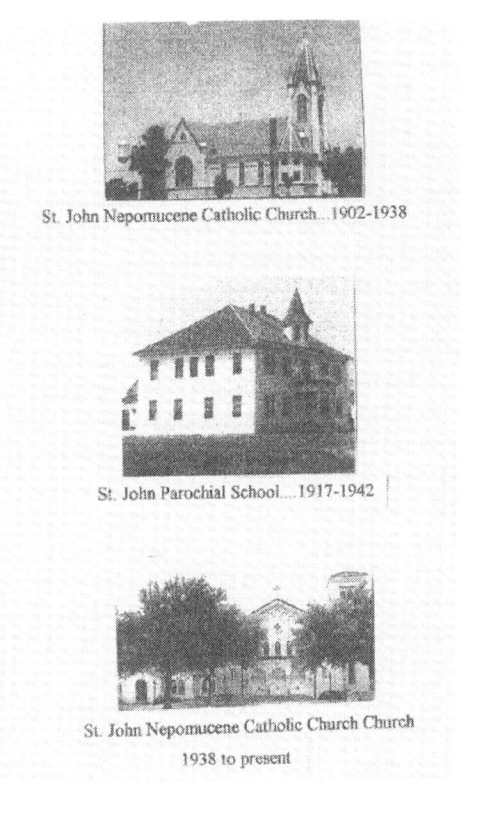

St. John Nepomucene Catholic Church 1902-1938

St. John Parochial School 1917-1942

St. John Nepomucene Catholic Church Church 1938 to present

equipped with double desks and each student had a seatmate. St. John's Church (the big, beautiful, present structure) was in the building process then; so a temporary building had been constructed for Church services. That's where I received my First Holy Communion. This temporary building afterwards, served as a school cafeteria for more than fifty years. (In the 1960's, my children ate their school lunches there.) Sending us to St. John's School was difficult for Mom and Dad. There weren't any school buses yet, so other means of transportation had to be arranged. Several of the neighbor kids, from down deep Creechville, rode with Mr. Frank Hubacek who had a car dealership in town. I think he deserved a medal for hauling this carload of kids to school. His wife, Beatrice Hubacek, was a teacher at Village Creek School and they lived across the road from the school. What I remember best about Mr. Hubacek was that he always dressed neatly. I usually had to sit on someone's lap directly behind him as he transported this carload of kids. He used a lot of nice scented talc, and I could see the telltale powder puff prints on the back of his neck.

Each school day at St. John's School began by going to church before classes commenced. On school days or on

Sundays, the boys always sat in the front pews on the right side of the church and the girls on the left. A Nun took her place behind each group ever vigilant to make sure they all behaved. If she saw any talking, snickering, or elbow punching, she got up from her place and walked over quietly and gently tapped the guilty one on the shoulder. Message received. To this day, I still sit on the left hand side of the church. We were never allowed to chew gum in church or in class. Each class began and ended with a short prayer. After the second grade at St. John's was completed, I returned to Village Creek School and continued there until I was ready for high school.

Mary Betik Trojacek

CHAPTER VI
PRAISE THE LORD

The majority of the Czech immigrants were religious and God-fearing people, and brought with them many traditional customs. Their religious fervor permeated their lives and was expressed in many ways ... even in the way they greeted each other. We grew up with those traditional phrases which came to us as easily and naturally as breathing or eating chicken noodle soup.

Hello ... This is the way this greeting was said ...

On entering the home of friends or relatives, the guest would say, "*Pochvalen Bud Pan Ježiš Kristus*," meaning, "Praised be Lord Jesus Christ." The host would reply: "*Až na věky věku, Amen,*" meaning, "Now and forever and ever, Amen."

Good-bye ... This is the way good-bye was expressed ... The departing guest would say, "*S Panem Bohem,*" meaning, "With Lord God." The host's reply would be worded the same, "*S Panem Bohem,*" also meaning "with Lord God." The inference was implied to mean, "God go with you", "God be with you," "God abide with you," "God stay with you," etc., whatever the intention of the one voicing the phrase. It was not uncommon to find a font of Holy Water on the wall by the door. Anyone who entered could bless themselves, for free.

On awakening on Good Friday, Mom reminded us of the Crucifixion of Christ. She would tell us to go outside to the water barrels on the sled and wash our face in the very cold water and offer it up for our sins. To us, this was true penance and could be likened to kneeling on a piece of split kindling wood.

The little *Kaplička* (miniature chapel) was a shining example of their love for the Blessed Mother. The little chapel must have been a wedding present to Mom and Dad, because I remember it being in the front bedroom forever and ever. It was about three feet high, two feet deep, and two feet wide. It was lined with light blue satin, and the statue of the Blessed Mother stood behind the glass door. All religious memorabilia were kept there such as blessed palms, rosaries, holy cards, etc., as well as a few items of value, like Mom's engagement ring and a $5.00 gold coin given to Mom and Dad for their wedding. The *Kaplička* stood on a little table overlaid with one of Mom's beautiful little table covers that she had embroidered when she was single and compiling her hope chest. Even though all of us kids shared the same bedroom and the room was always crowded, the view of the chapel was never obstructed. Whenever we entered the room, there seemed to be an aura conveying the message "best be good, she's watching!" The engagement ring got lost. The $5.00 gold coin is in Wesley's possession. He bought it from Mom in the 1970's. The *Kaplička* and the statue of the Blessed Mother? I don't know what happened to them.

Mom and Dad loved their God and His church. The large and beautiful stained glass window of St. John Catholic Church reflects their desire to keep the church beautiful. This window is on the right wall of the church, fourth from the statue of St. Theresa, the Little Flower of Jesus. The inscription on the window reads: In Memory of Joe and Frances Betik.

The walls in our home were adorned with pictures of the Holy Family, the Sacred Heart of Jesus, Mary the Mother of God, the Guardian Angel, and a few saints. A Crucifix was always in full view. These objects in display held a special meaning to all of us because most of the pictures had been wedding presents given to Mom and Dad in 1925. The dining table was the place for the Lord's bread. We were never allowed to sit on this table or put our feet or shoes on it.

When the weather was bad or Daddy was sick, we didn't go to church, but we didn't forget that Sunday was the Lord's Day. Sunday dinner preparations were made and while it was cooking, all of us knelt down and prayed the rosary. Mom led the rosary, the rest of us responded in unison. It was so hard to keep straight posture and so easy to slouch over the edge of the bed or chair. If the chair was really low, it looked like the person was praying on all fours. A Litany followed the Rosary. A Litany is a prayer arranged in a series of humble and earnest petitions asking for divine help and guidance in daily living. Usually we did our praying around 11:00 and the tantalizing aroma of chicken noodle soup drifted all through the house. It was hard to keep our mind on the prayers.

My Mom and Dad were lifelong members of the Czech Catholic fraternal organizations, namely the *K.J.T. (Katolicka Jednota Texaska)* which was for men, and the *K.J.Z.T. (Katolicka Jednota Žen Texaskych)* for women. Children were enrolled too. These organizations provided life insurance, spiritual and social benefits, and promoted fellowship and patriotism to their new country.

The Czechs had a special devotion to St. Joseph and on the eve of his feast day all the namesakes of St. Joseph and the Joseph derivatives were honored with a serenade. The namesakes included those who were named Josef, Joe, Joža, Joseph, Joška, Jodie, Jožin, and Pepik. A group of young men in the neighborhood went around the community carrying a banjo, a violin, a guitar, and an accordion. They stopped and serenaded at every house where there lived a namesake of St. Joseph. The inspired group sang and played to my Daddy every year. It was beautiful! When World War II broke out, all the young men went into the service and this custom was put on hold. When the war was over so were the serenades, because when the boys returned home, they were too busy raising families and making a living. The custom was never revived.

1938.......Bernard Joseph, Mom and Dad's sixth child

Bernard was born March 19, 1938, on the feast of St. Joseph, and thus was entitled to a serenade too. He was the last of my brothers and sisters to be born while we lived on Grandfather Marusak's farm. Mom had a very difficult labor, and it was more than *Stařenka* Betik could handle, so Dr. Story was summoned for assistance. After a near death experience, no more children were born at home. Daddy took Mom to the hospital when Wesley, Ella, Evelyn, and Bobby were born. Bernard was baptized Bernard Joseph. St. Bernard is his patron saint; Joseph is a namesake of Daddy and also because he was born on the feast day of St. Joseph. His farm name was Bernart, pronounced with a distinct roll of the r's. In school teachers called him Bernard and his friends called him Yogi, after baseball player Yogi Berra. Today his friends still call him Yogi, and we, his brothers and sisters, still roll the r's when we say Bernart. To his work crew he is known as B.J. (B for Boss or Bernard).

In 1938 Mother Cabrini became the first American saint. By now there were thirty-six million Americans on Social Security; minimum wage jumped to forty cents per hour and Joe Louis defended his boxing title. St. John Church (the present structure) was built. It was consecrated on November 15, 1938. Adolf Hitler promoted himself to Military Chief in Germany and started invading the neighboring countries. In February 1939 sadness and fear gripped Czechoslovakia, as the country was overrun by the Nazis; Czechs in America cried and prayed for their homeland and its people.

Bernard was about a year old and just crawling around, when suddenly he disappeared. Everyone searched frantically. We checked and rechecked the stock pond, the barn, the road, the fields . . . no *Bernart*. Finally, after a long search, he was espied way under the house surrounded by chickens. He was clad only in a diaper, and covered with drool and dust from the top of his head to the bottom of his feet. I don't recall who the hero was that found him. In those days, most of the farm houses were up on blocks, so there was lots of crawl space under them. Most of the houses did not have siding below the floor level so it was a haven for chickens in the summer as drafty breezes circulated underneath the house. For us, it made the house cooler in the summer and colder in the winter.

Bernard was in grade school when he became ill and was diagnosed with Rheumatic Fever. Along with other instructions the Doctor said he must be confined to bed for several weeks. Daddy slept on a pallet on the floor by

Bernard's bed in case he needed something during the night. At meal time Daddy carried him to the dining table or the food was brought to him. Mom and Dad followed Doctor's orders very carefully. The memory of Mom's nephew, 13 year old Frankie Marusak, who had died of the same illness, was still fresh on their minds. Bernard missed many school days, but lessons were brought home to him so he kept up with classes.

    Bernard married Nancy Kuchař and they have six children: Steve, Patrick, John, Andrew, Henry, and Damon.

CHAPTER VII
AN END TO SHARECROPPING

In 1939 the farm across the road from Grandfather Marusak's place came up for sale, and Mom and Dad proceeded to buy it. For them, that's when sharecropping came to an end. And it turned out to be quite timely too, because about this time, Grandfather Marusak had decided to turn his farm over to his youngest son, Frank, which meant that Mom and Dad and Uncle Joe and Aunt Agnes would have to move. This can be likened to Musical Chairs. Mom and Dad were moving from the pale green house to the farm across the road. Uncle Joe was moving his family from the two-story Marusak home to Telico. Uncle Frank was moving his family from Waxahachie to the two-story Marusak home, and my grandparents, Alois and Anna, were moving from the two-story Marusak house to the pale green house that we had just vacated.

The 130-acre farm that Mom and Dad were buying was owned by Rudolf Patak. Mom and Dad did not have enough money for the down payment as required by the Federal Land Bank, so they borrowed $300.00 from Aunt

Mary Patek and the same amount from Aunt Frances. I don't know what kind of arrangement was made for repayment, but I think Daddy forfeited his inheritance share to the home place on FM 85. Later, Aunt Mary and Aunt Frances bought Uncle Louis's and Uncle Frank's share, making them owners of the Betik farm.

At last, after fourteen years of sharecropping, having survived the depression and the flood, the serious bout with lockjaw, and having six little offspring running around, Mom and Dad moved from the pale green house to their own farm.

Our new house was set off the main road quite a piece and was almost obscured with five big cedar trees and two grand lilac bushes. (The house really wasn't new, but it was new to us.) The three spacious rooms accommodated all of us. Two double beds fit neatly into one bedroom. There was room for the *Kaplička*, a big antique dresser bureau and room to spare for other items like the armoire which we called *armara*. The living room served as Mom and Dad's bedroom and had a space for a wood burning heater with black stove pipes going up into the chimney. A mini clothes' line was strung close to the stove pipes. We did our homework at a large round table in this room. A kerosene lamp provided our light. The large country kitchen was combined with the dining room. There was plenty of room for a cook stove, a big dining table, and a long bench against the wall behind the table for the smaller kids to sit on. We didn't have cabinets, instead we had cupboards for the dishes. A *mukovnica* was a common kitchen fixture in the days of yore. It was a structure about four feet wide and three feet high, divided into three bins. One bin held one hundred pounds or more of flour, one held one hundred pounds or more of sugar, and the third was for our dish rags. By the door stood a little bench on which sat the water bucket with dipper and a wash pan. We had a *kumbalek,* that was a small storage room at the end of the screened porch for hanging winter coats, overalls, etc. A wide hallway connected the front porch and the back porch. Part of the back porch was screened and the rest of it extended on toward the well. A thick climbing rose bush wrapped itself around the frame of the well and rambled along the open side of the porch. It was pretty and also served as a shield from the cold north wind. Our new farm had hills and bottom land. The bottom land bordered Walker Creek; John M.

Vrla's farm was on the right, the farms of Frank Trpak and Richard Krajca were on the left, and the farm frontage went along the main road. The long dirt driveway led into our backyard. The entry was graced with the rose-covered well on the left and a salt cedar tree and two large vitex bushes on the right. The salt cedar bloomed in a delicate shade of pink and the vitex in a deep blue. They were a sturdy and beautiful compliment to our landscape. Today, their popularity has dwindled down, probably because they are deciduous. Note: After Mom sold the farm in 1971, I have not gone back to the home place. The house and the barn are still there, but the passing of time has dealt its toll. And I guess by now the picturesque salt cedar, the vitex and the lilacs have lived out their life span and are no longer there. The rose climber that once encircled the well continues to bring a nostalgic memory in living color. Today, a rose climber rambles along a fence in my yard; it's a starter from the one that once rambled on the well.

  The front door was rarely used; everyone entered through the back door. Anyone approaching the entry with muddy shoes or feet was obligated to scrape off all the mess before entering. A horizontal metal slat between two vertical posts driven into the ground was designed especially for this purpose, and every country home had one. It was called *škrabak*, meaning scraper. Everyone complied because no one wanted the wrath of the "Lady of the House" on them.

When we moved to this new house, Bernard was not quite two years old, and Wesley was on the way, scheduled to be born in August 1940 on our new place. We called this farm our home place, because all of us; my brothers and sisters, spent all, or a big percent of our growing up years, on this farm. Each of us cherishes a bundle of memories. After we moved to the new farm, Daddy's top priority was to construct a storm cellar. The cellar provided security and safety for the family, especially in the tornado season. He dug the excavation for the cellar by himself with a shovel, an aching back, and the sweat of his brow. The inside structure was overlaid with brick and concrete. Then he built wide shelves that served as beds because sometimes we spent the entire night in the cellar just riding out the storm. Mom kept her canned goods on the upper shelves. Most of the time it smelled damp and musty, in spite of the two vents to the outside. No one complained because we felt like it was a pretty fair exchange for safety. His design also included an emergency exit door but we never had to use it. The cellar accommodated the family, the dogs, and sometimes the neighbors too. Anytime the weather appeared threatening, off into the cellar we went, toting blankets and the kerosene lantern. Mom was not afraid of storms, so she was always the last one in. Before she took refuge in the cellar, she picked up the buckets in the yard rolling around with the high winds and gathered the clothes flapping on the clothesline. After Mom entered the cellar, the door was shut and anchored down.

The Storm Cellar

The lantern was hung on a nail on the bracing post, and the dim light gave us comfort as we listened to fierce winds, thunder and the lashing rain. I can still see Daddy sitting on the upper steps, raising the door a few inches every now and then, to see if the storm had abated. If he didn't see any signs of it letting up, he pulled the door down by a heavy chain, anchored it, and waited a while longer. We felt very fortunate to be in the storm cellar the night the winds ripped off part of the roof of our house, and picked the house up off the blocks and dropped it a piece away. Most of Mom and Dad's dishes and wedding china broke when the cupboard toppled over. Few pieces remained intact and Mom gave one piece to each of her daughters 40 years later. The house sustained a lot of damage, but neighbors got together and got busy. Neighbors helping neighbors.

The Way It Was

Before I proceed with the way it was back then, I'll comment on some perceptions and views that go through my mind as we begin a new era, the new millennium. Seventy years have passed, and as I reflect on those days of the way it was, I wonder how we would manage today if all of our "basic needs" were taken away. Could we draw water out of a well for all of our needs? Could we read or sew by the light of a kerosene lamp? Would someone be happy to get out of bed on a very cold morning and start a fire in the wood-burning heater? Go back to bed for a little bit until the room warmed up, then get up and find the fire had gone out? There are so many automatic appliances, gizmos, and gadgets we take for granted! We give very little thought as to how electricity, heat, and water are delivered to us, but we panic when it's not there at the push of a button. I remember when survival was possible without push buttons. I know . . . I was there.

Surviving without push-buttons

A kerosene lamp provided light at night. We usually had two lamps; one on the kitchen table and one in the family room (which was also Mom and Dad's bedroom.) Lots of homework was done by the dim light of a kerosene lamp. One of the chores that had to be done before sundown was to make sure there was enough kerosene in the lamp and the cylinder was clean. A cylinder smoked up and blackened with soot cut down on the amount of light the lamp provided. The glass cylinder was very fragile and had to be cleaned with the greatest of care. If a night light was needed, like when someone was ill, all we had to do was just turn down the wick, and the dim light got dimmer. Electricity was not provided to rural Creechville until the early 1950's. I was at St. Paul Hospital Nursing School then, and when I came home now and then, everything seemed so different. I mean you could really see. It was so bright.

    The ice box preceded the refrigerator. It was non-electric, and cooled most of the foods reasonably well. We did not have an ice box, but some country folks did and the Ice Man delivered ice every other day and placed a 50 pound block of ice into the top compartment. When Creechville was connected to electricity, it was not long before Mom and Dad, and everyone else got a refrigerator. The Fridge! What a wonderful and remarkable piece of an appliance! Such an easy way to chill milk, instead of putting a container of milk into the water bucket, and lowering it down into the well to cool it. We could now have bologna, cold milk, Jell-O, and on and on; even ice cubes for lemonade. For a long time the Old Timers referred to the refrigerator as the ice box, some still do. When all the rural households got a refrigerator like the town-folks, the Ice Man lost his job.

    In the rural areas, water was available from these

sources: cistern (rain water), artesian well (underground spring), stock pond, and above ground water collection tanks. Rain water was collected off roof tops during a rain and it drained into the well via gutters. Not enough rain meant not enough water. Water in an artesian well was supplied from an underground spring. Folks with such wells were more blessed because their wells did not run dry. Usually this water was high in mineral content which made it difficult to form lather and suds. Some farmers set up large above ground tanks and collected water off the roof tops of the barn and sheds. After a rain all the roof tops were clean. Stock pond water was brought in barrels placed on a custom-made sled. The sled was pulled by a mule team (tractor later). The barrels were filled bucket by bucket with water from the stock tank and on the way back to the house, we avoided going over terraces and prayed the mules would go straight and on even ground. If the barrels flipped over, we just had to make a U-turn, and go back for a refill. In order to conserve our drinking water in the well, the tank water was used for washing clothes, bathing, washing dishes, watering the chickens, etc. After the dishes were washed, the water was saved and poured into a five-gallon bucket, and then Daddy carried it out to slop the hogs.

Our drinking water was rain water and we drew it out of the well in a bucket attached to a long rope or chain. Anyone, family, friend or foe, as well as a guest, was welcome to a cool refreshing drink of water. Everyone drank out of the same dipper and dipped the water out of the same bucket which usually sat on a little bench by the back door. A wash pan sat next to the bucket. Life Buoy soap, Lava, or a wedge of homemade lye soap was nearby and a community towel or rag hung above on an old fashion coat hanger . . . a nail in the wall.

All the farmers had the same concerns about water. In 1963, those living in the communities of Creechville, Telico, Crisp, and Alsdorf, got together and petitioned the Farmer's Home Administration Office, to approve and assist in the construction of a water supply system to serve the needs of the rural community. Approval was granted and the work began. The project was completed in 1965 and the first water began to flow from the faucets. The water came from a public supply, was clean, safe, plentiful, and convenient. Just turn the tap and out comes running water! Before that, running water was defined as . . . you get a bucket of water and you run with it. We were never allowed to waste water, and Mom and Dad never overcame the deeply ingrained serious appreciation for water, even after it was more abundantly available. Mom

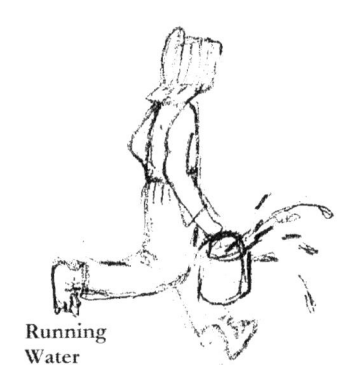

Running Water

especially thought it was so wasteful to run the water into the sink to get a cup of hot water. She felt there were four or five cups of water wasted before one cup of hot water was obtained. She heated her cup of water on the stove. It wasn't the cost of the water that bothered her; it was the water that was being wasted. Water indeed, was a precious commodity, and the struggling farmers depended on God's goodness to send them timely rains. Not a drop of water was ever wasted, no matter what source it came from.

Saturday night baths took place in a galvanized #3 wash tub on the screened back porch, or by the kitchen stove in the winter. Everyone took a bath in the same water. The energetic one who set it up usually was first. Hot water was added from a pot on the stove. After all the baths were taken, the tub was carried out and the water poured on a fig bush, rose bush, or other plants.

An outdoor privy, a two-holer, was available year round, but no one lingered too long in the winter time. I never understood why most of the family outhouses were two-holers

Out back...

and were still called a privy, except maybe for private companionship? And one could always see out through the moon shaped cut-out on the door and anyone on the outside could also look in, but it was still called a privy.

The source of heating came from a wood-burning heater, and meals were prepared on a wood-burning stove. It was necessary to have a brisk fire in the stove in order to create enough heat to bake bread. We always had to make sure the *tsuk* (a damper on the side of stove pipe) was positioned so the heat was directed into the oven instead of going up the chimney. We had fresh homemade bread 'most every day, but somebody had to bring in the wood. Often someone would spout "It's your turn to bring in the wood!" An armload or two had to be brought in every day. It was put in the wood-box behind the stove. In the 1950's, Mom and Dad stepped up in household conveniences and got a new kitchen stove fueled with propane gas, but continued to heat the house in the winter-time with firewood.

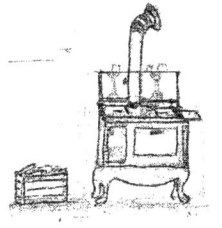

Washing clothes was an all day affair, once a week, usually on Saturday. First, the water was hauled in from the stock tank, and then the black *kotel* was filled with water. The water soon heated as a brisk fire under the *kotel* was kept up with wood from the wood pile and the debris and trash picked up in the yard. Meanwhile, two or three large tubs were set up. Tub #1, with wash board and a generous wedge of homemade lye soap was for hot water. Stubborn stains and ground in dirt got an extra lather of the soap and scrubbed more vigorously. Leaning over the scrub board brought on an aching back and sore knuckles. The clothes were rinsed in 2 or 3 tubs of water. All the clothes were wrung out by hand and this procedure developed strong wrists, hands, and arms, especially when wringing out bed sheets, overalls, and large shirts. These large pieces of laundry retained a lot of water, and when they were hung out, the clothes lines sagged with the weight of the saturated clothes. Sunday clothes, pillow cases and such, were dunked in a bucket of starch then hung out. The scrub board was put aside when we acquired our first washing machine. This washing machine would be a real antique today. It was a deep tub mounted on four legs, and had a handle mounted on the side. This handle was pushed back and forth causing the agitator to move the clothes about in the tub. The speed cycles were determined by the operator. I was about 10 years old and I recall having to do this chore many times . . . push, pull, push, pull. It was monotonous but better than the scrub board. This machine was also equipped with roller wringers and they too were manual. A year or two later we advanced

to a gasoline powered washing machine (no electricity yet). The clothes were agitated automatically now and we no longer got the hand and wrist exercises from wringing out clothes. All we had to do was poke the clothes into the non-stop-rolling wringers. We were always cautioned to keep our fingers, our bonnet strings, and our hair out of the grasps of the wringers. When one got caught, the wringers didn't stop, they just kept on rolling, then . . . too bad, so sad. No modern clothes dryer, so we continued to dry our clothes the old fashion way . . . on the clothes' line in the sun and the wind. It could be called the Solar Clothes Dryer. After electricity was extended deep down Creechville (1950), Mom stepped up again, and got an electric washer with wringers. This washing machine made our wash day a picnic. Still no running water, so we had to prepare the water as before and we continued to use our solar clothes' dryer. There were so many clothes to hang out to dry, we ran out of line space and hung them out on the garden fence. When all the laundry was done, the water was carried off to water Mom's flowers, fig bush or which ever plants needed water the most.

Mom made her own lye soap. All I know, it takes old lard, a little water and a can of lye, but I don't know the ratio.

If anyone is interested in the recipe, ask my sister Lillie, she makes it every once in a while. Also, you might ask if the results are better if the soap is made by the signs of the moon, for Stařenka would have said that the "sign of the moon" was the secret ingredient in making a successful batch of homemade lye soap.

Ma Bell had not made it to the country yet, so no one had a telephone.

The phrase T.G.I.F. had not been coined yet that we knew of, but we looked forward to the weekend as much as any modern nine to fiver. For us, Sunday was a designated day of rest.

Country Saturday

Going to town on Saturday was the way many country folks socialized. They visited old friends and made new ones in the stores, on the sidewalks or in the streets. If the kids had a dime in their pocket, they went to see a picture show. There were two theaters in town, the Plaza and the Grand. Admission charge was ten cents; a few years later, it skyrocketed to twenty-five cents. Our family seldom went to town on a Saturday just to while the time away. After spending Monday through Friday in the fields, this was our day to catch up on house chores, mopping the floors and the porches, changing bed sheets, and washing and ironing clothes. We usually baked one or two pies or cakes for Sunday. One kid had to shine all the Sunday shoes. Sunday shoes were for church and special occasions only. Each one of us had a pair, so there were many pairs lined up on the front porch (That was my favorite place to shine Sunday shoes). Another kid did the ironing and got each one's clothes ready for Sunday church. This was the time before perma-press fabrics, so we had to iron all of our Sunday clothes. We ironed and pressed the clothes with an iron powered with gasoline. The iron had a reservoir, the size of a cup, that was filled with gasoline and a little lever was turned which permitted the gasoline to enter the appliance, then it was lighted with a match. If the reservoir was overfilled, the drips of gasoline caught on fire too. I wonder why it never blew up.

Country Sunday . . . A day of rest.

So you can see that most of our Saturday was spent getting ready for Sunday. Sunday morning we put on our

Sunday dress, Sunday shoes, and a hat. In my growing up years, it was a church rule that all women and girls had to have their head covered when they entered the church. The present young generation will never see such a display of color and styles of hats: fancy hats, expensive hats, copycat hats, original hats . . . the millinery business flourished. In our little town of Ennis, there were stores that sold hats only. After the church relaxed the law and Catholic women stopped wearing hats to church, the hat business went downhill. The older ladies usually wore a *Babuška* or a *Šatka,* (similar to a head scarf), triangle shaped and tied under the chin. Some were very colorful heirlooms brought over from the old country. If a girl found herself in a situation of no hat, cap, or scarf, especially on school days, she could always get by, by pinning a hankie or Kleenex on top of her head. During the transition phase of going from hats, to no hats, prayer caps and mantillas were used by those who had a difficult time adjusting to the new concept. But after they got used to the idea, the prayer caps and mantillas were folded and put away in a drawer too. The men's attire was not complete if they didn't wear a hat with their Sunday suit. It could have been a Derby, a Stetson, a Fedora, or the type popularly worn in the prohibition days; but no matter what kind it was, it was removed before entering the church. They also removed their hats or caps when entering a home, whether his own, or anyone else's. And they never sat down at the dinner table with their hat on, for fear their Mama would knock it off. Men just didn't sit down to eat wearing a hat; however, most of them had no problem conforming because of early training and example.

In the summer it was best to go to an early Mass before it got too hot. Air conditioning was not available yet, so the only means of cooling was with a hand-held, hand-operated cardboard fan. A picture of a saint graced one side of the fan and an advertisement of the local funeral home was on the other side. The fans were strewn in the pews, and people could use them when the opened windows failed to draw a breeze. They were free; however, I feel that the funeral home got paid later . . . in due time, at the proper time.

In church, the kids sat in the front pews; Daddy sat midways on the right because he could hear better there; and Mom in the back, usually on the left. The pews in the back were reserved for mothers with babies and small children.

Today these pews are overcrowded; occupied mostly by those who want a quick escape or fast exit when Mass is not quite over. Parents with babies and small children go up front. Mass was in Latin, and the sermon in Czech. In the 1960's Mass changed to English.

The opened windows invited a bird or two and the kids in the front pews acted like they had never seen anything as funny as a bird in a church. The nun sitting a few pews behind them was kept busy.

Anyone wishing to receive Holy Communion fasted from food and water from midnight on. (Church law then; amended later.) There was not a better way to exercise self-discipline than to say "no," to a cobbler, cake, pie, or kolačky, sitting temptingly on the kitchen table before going to church. After Mass, the people gathered in groups outside and visited; sometimes for one to two hours. I think that my folks and our Marusak relatives were the best in the parish about visiting in the parking lot. This was a social affair for them. While they were exchanging bits about the weather, news, and local gossip, the kids took this time to run across the street to Honza's grocery store. We were starving, as we had fasted since midnight. We bought a package of six big fat cinnamon rolls, generously glazed with icing, for six cents.

My aunts and uncles and their families took turns visiting each other's homes on Sundays. Uncle Louis Marusak lived in Bardwell, and we looked forward to visiting with their children. On these occasions, we loved to go down to the pasture and go crawfishing or play on the *Rača*. The Rača (pronounced Racha) was a sort of playground equipment constructed by Uncle Louis where one end of a long 2 by 12 board was attached to an axle and anchored on to a pivot. The other end was connected to a wheel. It went 'round and 'round, and 'round, pivoting on the center structure; some kids pushing, some riding and everyone taking turns.

We enjoyed going to Uncle Frank's too, because they had a big slide, like the schools had, and they also had a bicycle. We didn't get to visit too often because they lived further away in Waxahachie. When Uncle Frank Marušak and his family moved to the Marušak Homeplace on FM 1181 across the road from our new farm, they still were the only ones we knew of who had a slide and a bicycle. Country kids did not have an outdoor gym set, but often a tire swing could be seen hanging off a tree in their yard. The beat-out turf underneath the swing was undeniable proof that the tire was not idle. Bicycles were becoming popular, especially among city kids, and as country kids got more oriented to the outside world, they started saving their cotton picking money so they could buy one too. Our first bicycle had no tires or brakes.

After Uncle Joe Marušak and his family had to move from the Marušak Homeplace, they moved to Telico. We missed them a lot as we had spent a lot of time together during the seven years of sharecropping and we were more like brothers and sisters. So now, when we had a yearning to see them, we walked all the way to Telico, (five or six miles), spent the night; stayed a couple of days, and then hiked back home. I was about ten or eleven years old.

Aunt Mary and Uncle Frank Salik had four boys and we got along well with our cousins and always had a good time when we went there. They lived in Alma, and the best time we had was when we went to help them pick cotton. Usually we spent a couple of days and nights. Kmotřenka (Godmother) loved to bake sweet treats for us and baked cookies, muffins, and made candy. She had a sweet tooth too, so she was happy to have the chance to cook it up a little. Uncle Frank and Aunt Mary Salik were godparents for all of Mom and Dad's children, and respectfully, we addressed them as Kmotřenka and Kmochaček. That put them on a pedestal above Auntie and Uncle.

1940 Wesley was the first to be born on our new home place, August 27, 1940

In baptism, Wesley Louis was named after St. Wenceslaus a much honored saint in Czechoslovakia, and also after Great-grandfather Vaclav Bětik. Louis is a namesake of Grandfather Alois Marušak. When Wesley was a youngster we called him Duke because he had frequent tantrums, and during these spells he wailed and howled and sounded like the neighbors' hound dog named Duke. His farm name was Venda or Venus and the sometimers called him properly, Vaclav. In school he was known as Wesley. In 1940 Franklin D. Roosevelt was elected to third term as President of the United States, and this same year, Winston Churchill became Prime Minister of Britain. German girls were ordered to save hair from haircuts to make felt. All of Europe was besieged by war and in Dunkerque, 340,000 allied troops were saved from annihilation. The first military draft number was drawn in the United States.

After Wesley (born in 1940), Ella made her debut in 1942; Evelyn 1944; and Bobby 1946. Mom and Dad allowed us older kids to select the name of each newborn. In 1959, Wesley married Vera Kriska and they have three children: Kevin, Dwayne, and Kenneth.

1940 Continued

Now that Mom and Dad had their own farm there was so much they wanted to do with it, but didn't have enough money to do it with. Each year after the crop was harvested, the crop yields paid off the bank note, and then Dad borrowed again to put the next crop in. Each year was a gamble. We lived harvest to harvest; nine-to-five folks live paycheck to paycheck. But Mom and Dad were good managers, skilled in improvising and doing without, and used their talents to diversify; so in a few years the farm was paid for. They paid in cash for all household and farm needs at the time of purchase. If they couldn't pay for it, they didn't need it badly enough. We were always saving, and most of the things we didn't need, we did without. Not just material things, but even entertainment, like the two great movies that premiered in 1940, "The Wizard of Oz," starring Judy Garland, and "Gone With the Wind," with Clark Gable and Vivian Leigh. We didn't need to see them then so we didn't, but I did see them about twenty-five years later.

    The country was slowly recovering from the depression years, but we were so accustomed to scratching and saving, it was hard to throw anything away. In the "War" years ('41 to '45), people saved everything, hoarded what they could and just did without.

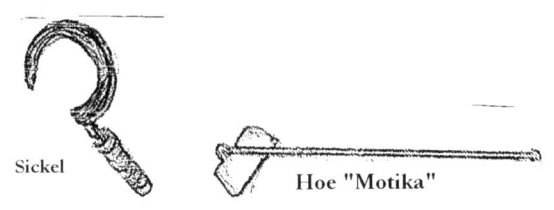

Sickel

Hoe "Motika"

Hay Rake "hrabe"

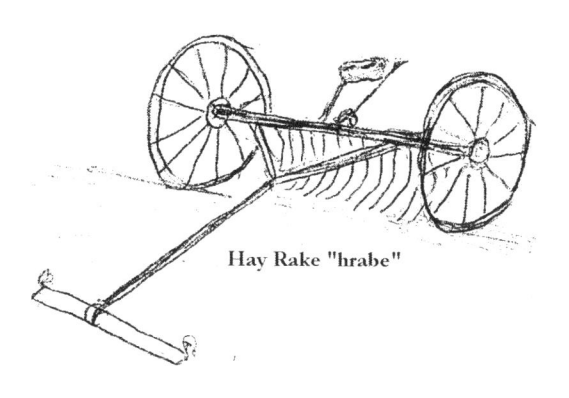

Mulberry Tree   Barn on our homeplace

CHAPTER VIII
THE TROJACEK FAMILY

At this point, I will enter some interesting notes about Jerry's roots and how Jerry Trojacek came to be. I enter them at this time because 1941 was when I first learned that Jerry and the Trojacek family existed. This chapter will be devoted to Jerry's Roots, the Vrla and Trojacek family history. Jerry and I were married in 1950, and in time had seven children; therefore, Jerry's family roots are also my children's family roots. This chapter is written especially for my children.

The information I have about Jerry's maternal roots is limited. Some of the facts were obtained from a research done by Jerry's aunt, Lillie Vrla Kucera and her family, who lived in Bryan, Texas. Their manuscript was titled, "*John M. and Mary Taraba Vrla Family History.*" In 1986 Aunt Lillie gave us a copy of the documented history. The information presented here is taken from this history and I believe it to be factual. The notes dealing with events from 1941 up to the time when Jerry's parents passed away are my observations during that pertinent time and it is written the way I saw it and as I remember it. Here again, other folks may have interpreted it or seen it differently.

John M. Vrla, *(Jan* in Czech, pronounced like Yon)

Jerry's maternal grandfather, was born October 12, 1868, in Želechovice, Moravia, Czechoslovakia. This little village was only a few miles from the city of Zlin, and was in the same vicinity from whence my ancestors came (Bětik, from the village of Březuvky, Sedlař from Doubrovy, Marušak from Provodov). As a young man, John worked in a shoe factory as an apprentice to a cobbler. As mentioned before, the youth in the old country were trained in some skill besides knowing how to till the land. Most farms were so small, it was impossible to support a family, even if one was fortunate enough to own a few acres. The town of Zlin was known as the boot center of Europe, where many boots and shoes were made and many cobblers were trained. *Bata*, the world-famous shoe factory, was located in Zlin. Not wanting to be a boot maker all his life, John was reading and listening to what people were saying about America. He was 19 years old, mature, and adventurous. A new chapter in his life began on June 10, 1887, when he went to Bremen, Germany, arranged for passage, boarded the ship named *Salle* and was on his way to America. It is not documented if he came alone or with family, but it was not unusual in those times for young people to make daring decisions and venture out on their own; even sail solo to lands unknown, and not have a clue as to what the adventure might bring. The idea being, "What have I got to lose?" The *Salle* sailed to New York first, unloaded and loaded cargo, and then went on to Galveston. After arriving in Galveston John checked in, complying with immigration rules, then went on to the Ennis area and commenced to work on his dreams. He was ambitious, worked hard and began to acquire land.

Note: There were many ships that transported immigrants to the new world. I found the recorded names of 51 ships. *Salle* was not on the list. However, *Halle* appeared several times. This is not to say *Salle* did not exist. It's also possible that it was a typo error in records. I mention this for the benefit of serious genealogists in the family who wish to further their research.

Mary Taraba Vrla, Jerry's maternal grandmother, was born August 12, 1867 in Rattaje, a village near the city of Tabor, in Bohemia, Czechoslovakia. Mary came to America in 1885 at age 18, with her parents František and Kateřina

Taraba, and her younger brother Joseph, age nine. The Taraba family came to Ennis two years before the arrival of John M. Vrla, who later became Mary's husband.

John and Mary met, courted and were married. They began their life as Mr. and Mrs. John M. Vrla in the Creechville community and settled on the land he already owned. This was their homeplace and they never moved from it. While they lived on this farm, nine children were born to them. Eight grew up to adulthood; one died when only two months old. John and Mary knew how to work and acquired more farm land. Eventually their estate totaled over 300 acres. In those days when success was measured by land ownership, this was quite an acquisition of assets. They worked the land, raised their family and were stable residents in the Creechville community the rest of their lives.

Jerry's grandmother died in her home March 15, 1935, and is buried at St. Joseph's Cemetery, Ennis, Texas. She was 68 years old. By this time, (in 1935), the family was grown and Grandpa, (*Dědeček*) did not need all this land, so six years after Grandma (*Babička*) died, he sold one of his farms to Jerry's Mom and Dad. This farm was located just across the road, due east from his homestead. The money

Grandpa received from the sale was divided equally among his children. Grandpa retained the Vrla Homeplace and continued to live there with his youngest son Willie and his family. Later, this farm and homestead were willed to Willie. (John M. Vrla was an honored guest at Jerry's and my wedding in 1950. I never knew Jerry's other grandparents.) Grandpa Vrla died December 02, 1957, and is buried alongside his wife Mary, at St. Joseph's Cemetery, Ennis, Texas.

Here is more information taken from the family history documented by Aunt Lillie Kucera. Grandma's brother, Joseph Taraba (1875-1960), who came to America with the family when he was nine years old, later married Elenora? (1876-1944) and they had two sons, Josef and Frank Taraba. Josef, born September 2, 1900, died when he was only nine years old on December 16, 1909, due to diphtheria. Frank J. Taraba (1901-1961), grew up to adulthood and married Mary E. Spaniel (1903-1996). They lived in the Creechville area for a few years and I remember going to school with their children, Frank Jr. and Agnes Taraba (Nekuza.). Their father and Jerry's mother were first cousins. Many years later, Frank Jr. and Jerry discussed this relationship and concluded they were second cousins, a fact neither one was completely aware of before. This discussion took place in Europe in 1993, when Frank Jr. and his wife Agnes, and Jerry and I, happened to be in the same tour group and toured Europe together for three weeks. We had a fabulous time.

Grandpa Vrla had one sister, Veronika Vrla (1859-1925). The circumstances of her immigration are not documented. Veronika married Frank Juriček and they had five children. Presently, the Juričeks living in the Ennis area are related to Jerry (2nd cousins). I have no other information on the Vrla family history.

All the deceased family members mentioned above are buried at St. Joseph's Cemetery, Ennis, Texas.

Listed here are the names of the nine children born to John M. and Mary Taraba Vrla, all born on the Vrla homeplace in Creechville:

1. Mary Vrla, their first child, was born October 13, 1892 and died February 24, 1971, age 78. Aunt Mary married Henry Kovarnik and they had four children: Mary, Hilda, Millie, and Henry. Jerry has lost contact with these cousins except the family of Millie, who married Frank Noska. Millie

has passed away but her family lives in the Dallas-Ft. Worth area.

 2. Frances Vrla, (Jerry's Mom), their second child, was born April 2, 1895 and died July 30, 1959, age 64. She married Anton J. Trojacek and 13 children were born to them. They will be introduced to you later in this script.

 3. Frank L. Vrla, their third child, was born on January 22, 1897 and died September 29, 1932, Age 35. Uncle Frank married Albina Kouba and they had two sons, Raymond and Milton. Albina died in 1923 at age 25. Milton was three years old and Raymond was five. In 1926, Uncle Frank remarried. His second wife was Mary Hrbacek and four children were born to them: Libbie, Georgie, Emil B., and Frank L. Jr. (Frankie). Uncle Frank and Mary Hrbacek were married only seven years when he died (1932) leaving Mary, now a widow, with six small children to raise. Raymond died in 1933, age 15. Milton and Frankie live in Ennis, Texas. Jerry sees these two cousins frequently, but has lost touch with the other cousins from this family.

 4. Karolinka (known as Carrie), their fourth child, was born on December 2, 1898 and died August 16, 1976, age 78. Aunt Carrie married Anton Galetka, who died at age

55. They had six children: Stanley, Joe, Libbie Abbie, Anton, Miroslav, and an infant daughter who died when she was only one week old. (Suzie Galetka Betik is Aunt Carrie's granddaughter. She is married to my nephew, Steve Betik). All of Aunt Carrie's children are deceased.

5. Joe Vrla, their fifth child, was born September 17, 1901 and died April 11, 1969, age 67. Uncle Joe married Helen Matous and they had three children: Helen Jo, Stanley, and Rose Ann. Helen Jo has passed away. Jerry stays in touch with his cousins Stanley and Rose Ann (Parma).

6. Johnny, sixth child, was born April 25, 1904 and died June 29, 1904 when only two months old.

7. Willie J. Vrla, their seventh child, was born January 11, 1907 and died June 5, 1979, age 72. Uncle Willie married Emilie Skrivanek and they had four children: Emilie (McElroy), Willie Mae (Mraz), Betty Jo (Culpepper), and Rose Ann (McClung). Willie Mae has passed away. Jerry stays in touch with remaining cousins.

8. Lillie, their eighth child, was born September 13, 1909 and died February 1998. Aunt Lillie married Martin Kucera and they had three children: Martin Dennis, Alvin J., and Mary Elizabeth (Hovorak). They live in Bryan, Texas.

This is the family that compiled the Vrla-Taraba family history. Jerry sees his cousins on special family occasions.

9. Kristina, their ninth child, was born April 22, 1912 and died . . . an exact date not known to me. Aunt Kristina married Robert Gaida and then moved to Dallas, Texas, where they lived the rest of their lives. Both are now deceased. They had two children: Robert Jr. and Linda. Jerry has lost touch with these cousins.

Voyage to America . . . Trojaček . . . 1901

John (*Jan*) Trojaček - (January 05, 1853 - July 08, 1916 . . . age 63).

Marie Helm Trojaček - (December 08, 1851 - October 17, 1936 . . . age 84).

John and Marie Helm Trojaček, (Jerry's paternal grandparents) were born, grew up, and were married in Bohemia, Czechoslovakia. At the time of their immigration they were living in Bechyne, a little village close to the town of Tabor. When they set out on their voyage, John was 48, and Marie was 49 years old. Their family consisted of five sons: Frank, who at that time was 23 years old; John was 20; Josef was 18; Anton was 11, and Karel was eight. The

Trojacek family sailed on the ship named *Norderney*. They came on the same ship with my Betik grandparents, and arrived in Galveston, Texas on June 27, 1901. After they got off the ship they were screened and documented. They complied with all the rules of immigration, and in doing so were faced with unfamiliar surroundings and customs, a language they could not speak, and people they did not know. Their planned destination was Ennis, Texas. I assume they went by train and upon arrival to Ennis, settled down and commenced to farm. Application for United States citizenship was accepted, and on September 25, 1906, they received their important documents . . . naturalized US citizens. Josef Novy served as witness. When John and Marie came to America, their oldest son, Frank J., age 23, stayed behind and followed two months later. He was independent and living in Raditice, Bohemia. His life took a new course when he boarded the ocean liner *Norderney,* and arrived in Galveston on August 29, 1901, the same ship as his parents but on the next round trip. He did not settle with the family, instead his ambitions took him to Bremond, Texas, where he married and raised his family. Mary Trojacek Novak, Jerry's first cousin, was the oldest of Frank's thirteen children. After she married, she lived in Ennis and my children always called her "Aunt Mary Novak."

John and Marie saved their money as they sharecropped, and in a few years realized their dream of owning land. They bought a farm in Telico which remained in family hands 100 years.

John (*Jan*), died July 8, 1916; Marie Helm Trojaček, died on Oct. 17, 1936. Both have been laid to rest in the Trojaček family plot at the Crisp Cemetery, Ennis, Texas. It's a large plot and other family members have been buried there since then, namely: Jerry's uncle, John F. Trojaček, who died in 1957; Jerry's Mom and Dad and their four infant children, and later in 1974 Anton A. (Jerry's brother), and in 1996, Albina (Jerry's sister).

It could be said that Anton J. Trojaček, Jerry's father, was a world traveler one hundred years ago. Not many eleven year old kids in the present day can say that, or can say they had the experience of rocking in a boat for three weeks while crossing the Atlantic Ocean. In this adventure and as a teenager, he met enormous challenges and was subjected to the many unkind realities of life as he helped his parents in resettlement. He learned responsibility early and in 1910, at the ambitious age of twenty, bought a farm in Telico, built a house, and lived there alone for two years. Growing cotton was his main crop. Telico was a little community northeast of Ennis. A creek called Village Creek separated Telico and the Creechville communities. Anton's future bride, Frances Vrla, lived on the Vrla home-place in Creechville, about five miles south across Village Creek. Anton and Frances met

Anton J. and Frances Vrla Trojacek Wedding Day, August 27, 1912

and their acquaintance blossomed to courtship, and the courtship led to matrimony. They were married on August 27, 1912. Anton J. was twenty-two years old and Frances was seventeen. They began their life as Mr. and Mrs. Anton J.

Trojaček in Telico, in the little house he had built. As the family grew, they built a new and bigger house with the proceeds of a bountiful cotton crop. They had thirteen children born to them, four died in infancy. Mary Novak, Jerry's cousin, assisted with some of the home births. The nine children who grew to adulthood were: Anton A., Willie, Leslie, Victor, Janie, Albina, Jerry, Adolf, and Otto. They lived on this Telico farm and attended Telico School District # 81, until 1941, when Anton J. and Frances bought the farm from her father, John M. Vrla, and moved to Creechville. They retained the Telico farm, and when their son Willie returned from the Army in 1945 and married Viola Honza, they started their married life on this Telico farm and raised their nine children in the house Willie's parents built in 1922.

My first contact with the Trojaček family was in 1941 when their kids entered Village Creek School. That's when I first met Albina, Jerry, and Adolf (Otto was only four and had not started school yet.) Jerry was in the fourth grade, and the whole class was impressed on how smart he was. In Geography class, Mrs. Stout, our teacher asked, "How many counties are there in the State of Texas?" Jerry was the only one who raised his hand. He came forth with the right answer; "254." Jerry and Adolf were the only boys in school who wore navy blue/white striped overalls. They were dressier than the common blue overalls, and seemed to convey an image of class. Jerry was a freckle-faced youngster with a mind of his own. His Mom called him Jarouš, (short for *Jaroslav*), but often she referred to him as Neřad, meaning a non-conforming rascal. It seemed uncomplimentary, but one could detect motherly love between the syllables. He was born at home in Telico, September 16, 1929, assisted by his cousin, Mary Trojaček Novak. He was baptized September 30, 1930. His baptismal certificate (in Czech) reads Jaroslav Trojaček. No middle name. Years later Jerry gave himself a middle name and is legally known as Jerry Allen Trojacek.

For some reason, Jerry's birth was never registered with the Bureau of Vital Statistics. He went to school, got a job, was given a social security number; enlisted in the U.S. Air Force at age 18, obtained a passport, and paid his taxes, and all without a birth certificate. In this present year of 2003, the only person living, who could attest that Jerry is indeed, Jerry Trojacek, is his brother Leslie, who celebrated his 86th birthday on April 18, 2003. In 1990, Leslie had the opportunity to vouch for Jerry's identity when Jerry applied for his passport. It was obtained without any problems. On this occasion Jerry and I had plans to go to London to attend the 40th wedding anniversary of Jim and Nancy O'Dell, Karen's Mom and Dad. (Karen is our daughter-in-law, married to our son, Gary). Today Jerry is going about his merry way with a personally-spun middle name but still without a birth certificate.

Anton J. Trojaček, Jerry's Father, as I saw him.... May 02, 1890 November 11, 1965 . . . age 75

Anton J. was a proud man. He always wore a hat and carried a cane (just for looks), especially in public. He sported a handlebar mustache, smoked a pipe, dressed neatly and looked quite distinguished. As in most Czech families, the father ruled the roost with a firm hand, and everyone in the family complied and accepted his decisions. He believed success was determined by land ownership and money in the bank. Membership and active participation in the Czech organizations was important to him and he encouraged his kids to do the same. Frances didn't have to worry about shopping, he did it all; from groceries, to household goods, to buying material for a new dress for the girls.

Anton J. Trojaček's family came from Bechyne, Bohemia, in Czechoslovakia, and I suppose that's where he was born. He never talked about the old country. I thought perhaps he feared the possibility of being reported to or being traced by the powerful Austro-Hungarian authorities because there they continued to enforce the strict military conscript of all teenage boys and it seemed to reason that an empire in conflict most of the time needed all the manpower it could get. As noted earlier in this writing, this was one of the reasons that caused many of the immigrants from Czechoslovakia to leave their country. Their boys were being made to fight for Austro-Hungarian interests, not for improving the lives of oppressed people in their own homeland. Anton's aim for keeping a low profile was to protect his family, for now, he too had sons. There were many other immigrants who felt they had to take measures and guard their identity; to make sure possible repercussions did not follow them. Some even changed their name; some spelled their name differently than in the old country, and some, like Anton J. Trojaček, just kept a low profile.

Beyond Ellis Island

Frances Vrla Trojacek, Jerry's Mother as I saw her.........April 03, 1895 - July 30, 1959 . . . age 64

Frances was a sweet lady who was a "Stay-at-home-Mom." She presented a true picture of a *Babička* (grandmother). Her long hair was brushed back and secured in a bun at the back of her head and her plump stature provided a very comfortable spot on her lap for her grandchildren. Family and friends who came to see her would find her most often in her favorite rocking chair in the family-room/bedroom. On the table behind her was a loud-speaking radio, and the family tried to keep up with the "war news." (Victor and Willie were in the service during the war.) While *Babička,* as her grandchildren called her, sat in her rocking chair, Dědeček (grandpa), parked his chair in the corner behind the cast iron heater, smoked his pipe, tended the embers, and put a log on the fire when needed. *Babička* was a great cook, but exercised her cooking skills best on holidays and on days when the boys were expected home on furlough. This was during the time when commodities were rationed and many items were very dear and sometimes hard to come by. Sugar especially was saved for these special occasions. The kitchen was the center of activity as Jerry's

Mom, Janie and Albie were busy making all kinds of goodies. So when there were so many tempting pies and cakes around, could anyone possibly miss one? Jerry speaks of how he confiscated one at such a time, and ate the whole thing behind the barn all by himself. He was about 12 years old. Probably no one ever missed the one he stole, but had his Mom known, she would have called him *Neřad* again.

Aside from special occasions, the farm menu didn't change much from day to day, or week to week, as long as the potatoes lasted. This was the common staple in most country households and many meals consisted of potatoes only; however, not all meals were meatless. When a dish of chicken was put on the table, there were just enough pieces to go around. Their meals were cooked on a wood-burning stove and the house was heated with a wood-burning heater. Usually bread was baked at the same time they did their ironing to get more benefit from the hot stove. They used the method of alternating flat irons heated on a hot stove. In the winter time the hot kitchen stove was nice and cozy, but in the summer the hot rooms just got hotter. One hot summer day I watched Jerry as he ironed his white shirt with the flat alternating irons. As I recall he did a good job, ironing the collar last. The Trojaček life style was similar to the Bĕtik's (my family), and not much different from all the other families living in the area. I don't remember that anyone lived in a brick house; all were frame houses built on blocks. The three to four rooms, including the kitchen, accommodated a large family. The Trojaček's house was a four-room square. You could walk from the kitchen into the living room/bedroom, to the next bedroom, and the next bedroom and then find yourself back in the kitchen where you started. The back porch was built around the well and no one had to go out in the rain or hot sun when drawing water. The front porch faced the main drag, (now called FM1181), and on this porch were a couple of rocking chairs and a cot where one could spend some leisure time, especially in laid-by season. Laid-by was a 2-3 week time after the hoeing of cotton was completed and picking cotton began. There really wasn't much to see even from these "front row seats." Traffic was very light. Most farmers went to town only when necessary and usually drove the same old pick-up or car for years. Teenagers didn't have a car, so they didn't cruise up and down the road. The postman went regularly and drove the same car day after day and could be identified from as far as you could see. Seeing a strange vehicle in the vicinity could mean a *Pedlak* was selling something or a new Romeo was romancing a lass somewhere down deep in Creechville. The Bětik's house, my homeplace, set off the road a little distance and we felt more isolated. We liked to visit with Janie and Albina (we called her Albie), and frequently sat on the front porch with them. The house was dismantled in the 1970's.

In the late 1950's Jerry's Mom was diagnosed with Leukemia; treatment was not successful, and she died July 30, 1959, at age 64. She died at her home, and is buried at the Crisp Cemetery. Mary Denise, my daughter, was born three months later, October 29, 1959 so she never knew her grandmother.

The house seemed empty after Jerry's Mom died. Jerry's Dad and Anton A. (Jerry's brother) continued to live on the family home place in Creechville, keeping each other company, tending to their cows, and doing a little farming.

In 1965, about six years after *Babička* died, *Dědeček* became very ill, and Dr. Dan Skrivanek came to the house to see him; then personally took him to the hospital. Immediate surgery was done, and they found a gangrenous gall bladder which had ruptured. In spite of the serious condition, *Dĕdeček* did quite well after his surgery and his discharge was being planned, but on the morning of November 11, 1965, he suffered a heart attack and died. He was 75 years old. Joan Elaine, my daughter, was 10 years old, and he died on her birthday. Betty Ann, (Otto's daughter), was born October 31, 1965, while her *Dĕdeček* was in the hospital recuperating after his surgery.

The following are some brief notes pertaining to the children of Anton J. and Frances Vrla Trojaček.

1. Anton A. (June 03, 1913 - July 21, 1974, age 61) Being the oldest of a large family, he put their interests before his own. Willie and Victor were drafted into the military and Anton ran the farm and looked after the family and before long, time just passed him by. He remained single and continued to live on the Trojacek home-place in Creechville. After his father died, he lived alone except for his cows and his dogs. He purchased the family farm, but did not get to enjoy it very long. He died seven years later, and is buried at the Crisp Cemetery.

2. Willie (May 21, 1915 - November 23, 1995, age 80). After World War II, he returned from the Army, married Viola Honza and they lived in the same house that Anton J. and Frances had built in 1922. Improvements were made as time went on. After Willie passed away in 1995, Viola continued to live there alone. Their children are: Evelyn (Cepak), Delores (Rejcek), Willie, Marvin, Robert, Barbara (Ludwig), Ernest, James, and Henry.

3. Leslie (April 18, 1917) He married Millie Patak on Valentine's Day in 1953. They live in Garrett on the Patak home place where Millie grew up. They have no children.

4. Victor. (December 23, 1918 - August 23, 1976, age 57). He served in the Pacific Theater during WW-II. Upon his discharge, he married Rose Marie Marusak (my cousin) and they had ten children born to them. They were living on a farm in Telico when he became terminally ill. Most of the children were quite small when he passed away and Rose Marie managed to raise her children and keep the family together. After the children were grown, she continued to live in the same house. My kids call her Aunt Rosie. Their

ten children, all grown now are: Rose Ann (Saxon), Victor, Larry, David, Kenneth, Carolyn (Joyner), Leon, Eric, Lydia (Hotop), and Benny.

    5. John. 5th child of Anton J. and Frances, (February 19, 1921. Died in infancy).

    6. Mary. 6th child of Anton J. and Frances, (1922. Died in infancy.

    7. Janie (May 17, 1923 - February 15, 2002 age 78). She married Bohumil (also known as Bob) Vrana, and they have one daughter, Frances Vrana Dover. Janie suffered with diabetes and stroke for about five years and resided in a local nursing home at the time of her death. She died one week after her brother Adolf. Bob had a farm in Garrett, but after Janie died, he went to stay with his daughter, who lives in town. (Bob's mother, Anna Sedlař (Vrana -Sulak), and my grandmother Marie Sedlař Bětik, were sisters).

    8. Albina (October 18, 1927 - July 26, 1996, age 69) She married Harry Schubrick and they had three children:

Mary Betik Trojacek

Harry Milton, Belinda (Hart), and Geraldine (Pruit). Albina's husband, Harry, died when the children were quite small, (preschoolers).

9. Jerry (September 16, 1929.) He married Mary Betik (that's me), and we have seven children: Donna, married Larry Isom; Gary, married Karen O'Dell; Richard, married Joni Carlat; Joan Elaine married Nick Wensowitch, Mary Denise, married Richard Bruce; Christopher (Chris), married Kay Roberts; and Jeffery (Jeff), married Melanie Moseley. We have nine grandchildren: Gerald Isom - married Jamie Bolen; Matt Isom; Shohn Trojacek - married April Johnson; Aaron and Audrianna Trojacek; Christian Whiddon and Austin Trojacek; Annie and Adeline Trojacek. Our great-grandchildren are Lucas, Juliana and Gregory Isom, and Lydia and Madiline Johnson, Hannah and Corbin Trojacek.

In 1980 we formed a family business under the name 9-T Farms Nursery (Nine Trojaceks). We're retired now and are enjoying our retirement. I love to dabble with oil painting and like to sew. Jerry takes time to give daily pep-talks to his herd of registered Angus cows. We both love to spend time with our children, grandchildren and great-grandchildren.

10. Adolf (July 08, 1932 - February, 08, 2002., age 69.) Adolf married my sister, Mildred, and they raised six children. They have lived on the "farm on the hill," since the 1950's after his discharge from the service. This land once belonged to Grandpa Vrla and is part of the farm purchased by Adolf's parents in 1941. Their children are: Danny, Janis (Wensowitch), Judy (Rickman), Marcus, Kathy (Rutherford), and Greg.

11. Anna, 11th child of Anton J. and Frances (December 31, 1934, died in infancy).

12. Johnnie, 12th child of Anton J. and Frances (March 25, 1936) died in infancy.

13. Otto (March 02, 1937 . . .) He married Irene Houdek and they had four children: Florence (Darst), Lawrence, Betty (Huffman), and Aaron. Florence, Betty, and Aaron have established homes on the Trojaček Homeplace. Otto and Irene divorced and Otto now is married to Jeannie Patterson.

Mary Betik Trojacek

Some interesting notes related to Jerry's Family . . . Vrla-Taraba and Trojaček-Helm

The lineage of the Trojaček roots has been traced to 1701. Research has been done by several Trojaček descendants.

The origin of the name Trojaček is derived from the name of a three-cent coin once used in the "old country."

John and Marie (Mary) were two of the most revered saints' names in the Czech heritage, and both sets of Jerry's grandparents were named in their honor: John M. and Mary Taraba Vrla, and John and Marie Helm Trojaček.

A brief summary on the lives of Anton J. and Frances Vrla Trojaček, including their wedding picture, can be found in the book *History of Telico, Texas*. It appears on page 252 and was submitted by a family member. Anton J. and Frances had 40 grandchildren, many great-grandchildren, and great-great-grandchildren, so Anton and Frances's legacy lives on. My children have 75 first cousins - 33 on the Trojacek side and 42 on the Betik side (Six of the 75 are double cousins).

It is interesting to note that my grandparents and Jerry's grandparents all came to America in the month of June: Bětiks June 1901, the Marusaks June 1902, the Vrlas

June 1887, and the Trojačeks June 1901. (The Trojaček and the Bĕtik families came on the same ship, the *Norderney*, at the same time. Jerry's Dad often mentioned it).

Clyde Barrow (of Bonnie and Clyde) was born in Telico, Texas; the same community as my husband, Jerry Trojacek. They never knew each other because Jerry was only five years old when Clyde met his fate in 1934.

In 2002 Ernest Trojacek (Anton J. Trojaček's grandson) bought the Trojaček family farm in Telico, and has built a beautiful home on it. It stands only a few hundred feet from the house built by Anton J. and Frances in 1922. In 2010 the farm will have been in family hands for one hundred years. Family farms that have been in the family for 100 years are being recognized by heritage societies all over the state, and Adolf and Mildred's farm has surpassed the century mark. Adolf's grandfather, John Vrla, bought it in 1890. In 1941 ownership was passed on to Adolf's Mom and Dad; and Adolf and Mildred acquired it in 1967. Today it is still in family hands. Grandpa Vrla's homestead and his remaining acreage were willed to his youngest son Willie, who then willed it to his four daughters dividing it into four sections. Today only two sections can claim a family legacy, because the other two have been sold to people outside the Vrla family.

A Trojacek Family Reunion is held every two years. This is an opportunity for all folks having a Trojacek connection to meet up and catch up on family news and happenings.

CHAPTER IX
THE 1940'S. OUR HOMEPLACE

"There's nothin' to do?" Anyone who has experienced life on the farm will agree that it was a never-ending cycle of work. It could be called: jobs, duties, tasks, or chores, but still work. Many of these tasks were boring and repetitious. The depth of boredom depended a lot on how one looked at it (attitude), or how well one could fantasize or daydream. Everyone on the farm was involved. Some of these tasks applied to the whole family; some to a select few, but no one felt left out. The fields were plowed and prepared for planting crops. A big garden was planted to provide vegetables for the table and surpluses for canning. Corn and cotton planted, cultivated, and hoed, then gathered in the heat of the summer. Hay was cut, baled and hauled; corn tops cut with sickle for fodder. And just when we thought we were laid-by after the hoeing season, it was time to gather the corn and put it in the barn, to be shucked later. Cotton was picked, and taken to the gin. No one had time to get bored. Firewood had to be cut and fences repaired. The cattle fed daily, as were the hogs and the chickens. Eggs were gathered, cows were milked, and hogs were slopped. No such thing as there's nothing to do. We found time to can and preserve fruits and vegetables, and made a lot of sauerkraut. In idle time, quilts were quilted, feathers stripped and made into pillows and featherbeds later. Old clothes were patched and mended. New clothes were sewed. One or two hogs were butchered and processed. Water hauled in from the stock pond, clothes washed and hung on the clothes' lines, ironed on Saturday if needed. Bread was baked 'most every day. Dinner interrupted 'cause there's chickens in the garden or cows in the corn. We did not need glasses to look for work. If we couldn't find something to do, we were sent out to chop the hateful white grass that persisted to flourish and multiply. It defied the poorest of growing conditions, and every year it was most bountiful under the clotheslines, around the wash house and in the orchard. We always called it white grass and could care less if it had a fancy botanical name. It was a given curse. Sundays were for going to church and visiting relatives, and in the evening, perhaps go to a dance at one of the local halls. On Monday morning, after a granted day of rest, Mom would awaken us, then come back a little later and find us asleep on our knees, slouched over the edge of the bed saying our morning prayers. We would have welcomed two Sundays in every week, one day to recover after a day of rest. Anyone who can picture himself in any of these life on the farm scenarios is bound to have a bit of country inside them. There were good times and bad times; times not so good, and times we could have done without, but we could laugh and Mom could sing and Dad, in his bib overalls, could tune us out as he relaxed in his favorite chair.

More about my parents, Joe and Frances Betik

My father was tall and lean, and his olive complexion just deepened in the summer from exposure to the sun. He had a full head of hair and combed it to the right, and it remained dark brown even in his later years. In his efforts to eke out a living while caring for his family, he had little time for dreams, but he did dream. On cold winter evenings, he would lie down on the floor with his back near the wood-burning heater, smoke his pipe and catnap. I think this was the time he dreamed, as his mind wandered into fantasy land, or he would work out problems or think about new ideas. I remember he visualized how some problem acres he had, could be converted into a productive project. This lowland acreage on the northwest side of our farm was adjacent to Grandpa Vrla's farm. All the surrounding hills drained down toward this area we called nižina, meaning lowland. When heavy rains came, these acres were submerged with rapidly flowing waters, washing away any crops. My father's dream was to build a dam downstream and contain all this water, thereby creating a huge lake. He planned to stock it with fish and promote it as a resort lake. It was a good dream with a lot of potential, but it never materialized.

  He was endowed with appreciation of nature and the love of the land, the rivers, the fields, and the woods. These gave him more pleasure than being surrounded by crowds of people. He was not a big talker, but rather enjoyed his quiet times. Honesty and integrity were at the top of his list of values, and all who knew him would agree that it was so. For a handshake from him was as good as a written contract. He was not a demanding person. The heel from a loaf of bread, and a cup of coffee would suffice for his breakfast and Mom never heard him complain about what was put on the dinner table.

While Daddy was easy going and liked to take time for simple pleasures like hunting and fishing, Mom's disposition was quite the opposite. She believed that time spent in non-productivity was time lost and could not be recaptured. According to Mom, idle time was wasted time. I think that sometimes her drive annoyed my father; he didn't like to be pushed. Mom's ideas transcended to us kids. When we were fooling around in the house and heard Mom or Dad coming, we quickly got busy doing something or anything, or just flew out the front door, because we did not want to get caught doing nothing.

Public image was important to Mom. Wherever we went, whether to church, to school, or to a dance, she wanted us to dress properly, and our behavior to reflect a little refinement. The hair had to be curled and combed, clothes clean and pressed, and we couldn't leave home without clean underwear. She felt that dressing sloppily, or behaving unruly in public, was a personal reflection on her. "What will people think?" or "What will people say?" I heard Mom say that so many times, it will stay with me forever. It didn't seem to be too important to Daddy, but I do remember a time when he was quite verbal about my appearance in public. I was about ten years old when we had gone to town and while I was sitting in the back seat I put on some bright red lipstick. He told me I looked like a monkey and wouldn't let me get out of the car until I removed it. We never saw Mom with her hair messed up. The first thing she did each morning was to comb her hair. She used to wear her hair shingled up in the back with a little wave and curl at the temples. Later when the *Toni* home permanent became popular, she had her hair curled. Her hair was dark brown too, and she was in her eighties before the first gray hairs began to show. I'm proud to say that I have acquired these particular genes from my Mom and Dad, because now at age 75, I do not have a gray hair on my head!

  Diversified farming, whether on a small or large scale, meant extra income for the family. Bee hives were part of the landscape on our farm as far back as I can remember. Daddy had several of these white custom-made bee hives scattered about on the farm, but most often he placed them close to the orchard and garden to make it easier on the bees to pollinate the fruit and vegetables. Bees were his pet project and he took diligent care of them. They provided several gallons of honey every year and we used it in cooking, with breakfast pancakes, or to treat a sore throat, especially if complimented with Dad's whiskey. For the Church Bazaar, Mom and Dad prepared jars of clear honey with a wedge of honeycomb in each of them, and then Mom would decorate them with red cellophane paper ruffled and placed under the jar ring. These attractive prizes were donated to the Bazaar. With Mom's ingenuity and artistic skills she could make anything look proud.

    The small herd of cattle that Daddy maintained was a source of pride to him and extra income too. It was distressing if one should die. So to prevent losses, Daddy learned as much as he could about taking proper care of his livestock. He acquired a lot of veterinary skills and knowledge from a local self-taught veterinarian, Jozin Krajca, who was big into veterinary medicine. As Daddy learned more and more about treating livestock, neighbors came to him and asked for advice about their sick animals. Daddy's cows enjoyed good health care and when one needed medicine, Daddy would put his hat on as he prepared to go to town, and say that familiar phrase, *"Toš musim jed to Apotheke,"* which meant "Well, I must go to the pharmacy." (Apotheke - universal for pharmacy). Later, in Czech-Tex lingo, we called the pharmacy *Drok Štora* which comes from the word Drug Store. Czech-Tex language is a fun language understood by all Czechs in America. It's a mix of Czech and English. By adding a Czech suffix to an English word, you can speak a dual language not found in any book.

    Daddy didn't neglect his mule team either. I remember the years when Daddy worked the farm with Rubik and Rudik; they were his work buddies. Together they plowed and bedded, planted and cultivated. We could see Daddy walking behind a plow or cultivator or other piece of farm equipment with the reins around the girth of his waist as he steered Rubik and Rudik. At the same time he kept his hands on the plow handles trying to maintain the right depth and the rows straight. Struggling with those farming methods, day after day, sunup to sundown, was an onslaught to the human body no matter how strong. No wonder he looked tired and weary when he came in from the field. At noon, he led the mules to the barn, took the bridle and the harness off, fed them, and let them roll around. After lunch while Daddy rested, one of us kids were sent to the barn to put the bridle and harness back on them and get them ready for the afternoon's work.

When Mom and Dad bought their farm, it had not been taken care of very well, and as a result the Johnson grass abounded from one boundary to the other. All of us were in the field sunup to sundown. Daddy plowing, cultivating, mowing and the rest of us hoeing. It seemed we never could get ahead of the tenacious Johnson grass. If our rows were especially tough, Mom stepped over on our row and helped us out. We could tell if one of the kids was exercising strategy, if he deliberately slowed down, or got to the end of the row with unusual speed. That meant only one thing, his eyes had already made a quick sweep of the next rows and he knew which turn-around-row was going to be tough and which one was going to be easy. He wanted the timing to be in his favor. We never could say we were "laid-by", a term applied to a short period of time after hoeing was completed and before cotton picking began. Our problem was we never got through with the hoeing.

There was so much work to be done that Daddy just could not keep up, so in the spring, he hired a person to help with the field work. We called this handy-man *Pacholek*. He lived with us on the farm and ate with us at the dinner table, but I don't remember the boarding arrangements. After about three spring seasons the kids were getting bigger and were of more help to Daddy, so the *Pacholek* lost his job on the Joe Betik farm.

A few years after we moved to our home-place, Daddy bought 112 additional acres which was adjacent to our farm, increasing his spread to 242 acres. It was about this time that Daddy bought his first tractor; a John Deere with lugs on the wheels. The tractor had a characteristic sound when it was in use. We called it "Poppin' Johnny."

Mom and Dad, and those still at home, lived on this farm through the 1940's, 1950's, and 1960's.

More about my Mom and Dad. Life on the farm and The Way it Was.

Mom and Dad enjoyed reading and subscribed to the Czech newspapers the *Našinec*, the *Katolik*, and the local paper *The Ennis Weekly*. They read them as well as the *Almanac*, and anything else they found from cover to cover. Although they had only a third grade education, they had a lot of self-learned knowledge. Realizing how important education was, they sacrificed a lot to give their children what they believed was best and sent all of them to St. John's High School, where all ten graduated. Mom and Dad hold this unchallenged record in the history of the parish school.

Mom had the attributes of knowing how to improvise, make do with what there was, and had a knack for creativity. Being a good seamstress, she could transform colorful flour sacks into attractive bonnets, aprons, or dresses. Our bed sheets and pillow cases were made out of flour sacks and the white ones served well as diapers. Flour and sugar could be purchased in 50 or 100 pound sacks in a variety of colors and patterns. When the seams were taken out, each sack provided about a yard or more of material. Mom always tried to get several in the same color and pattern. She did not knit or crochet but could do beautiful embroidery and fancy smocking. Her artistic work could be seen especially on christening dresses or other finery. The way she recycled clothes from Aunt Frances' Boss Lady would make one think she shopped far and wide for the fabrics to make our dresses. Even our Jewish dry-goods merchants in town were impressed. And as she sewed, she sang! Like most of the Marusaks, Mom was gifted with a beautiful soprano voice. She loved to sing, and sing she did! She sang while she sewed, she sang in the kitchen, she sang while washing clothes, she sang in the garden. Her favorites were mostly religious songs; songs that made you think of heaven. She sang songs of praise and thanksgiving; for even though times were not always good, she was thankful she had a good husband, a bunch of good children, a roof over her head, food on the table, and a place to lay down her tired and weary body. She also loved group singing and joined the happy choruses in any sing-along. With her brothers, they made the finest trio found anywhere. Her "singing genes" failed to be transmitted to any of her children. None of us are talented singers, but we can carry a tune, each his or her own. We can't sing very well, but we all can laugh! As the years went by and the family increased, laughter permeated the Joe Betik family and their humorous spirit created a climate of good times, comedy and clowning hilarity, many times Mom and Dad joining in. Here is an example of my Mom participating in an evening of fun. After the children were grown and on their own, Mom came to a costume party dressed as "Granny Clampit," a character in the Hillbilly TV show. She wore a silly little hat perched on top of her head, ankle-length dress, high-top shoes, and carried a roaster pan covered with the lid. A gasp escaped from each curious guest each time the lid was raised; looking back at them was a road-kill possum still in its natural state.

Even though Dad enjoyed a bottle or two of his own home-brew beer (he didn't make it all the time), he picked up a case of *Pearl* beer when he made an occasional trip to Dallas and it would last him quite some time. Mom didn't care for beer, but she enjoyed a glass of *Mogan David* wine. At special times like Mother's Day, Valentine's, Christmas, or her birthday, whenever someone gave her a bottle of *Mogan David* wine, she felt special.

From Mom we learned to play the domino game of "42", a good game of strategy. Wolf and Sheep was also a good game to play, especially on cold and rainy days. Wolf and Sheep was a form of checkers involving a diagramed sketch on a board about 18 x 18 inches. The idea was to move twenty sheep (white buttons), along lines from one side of the board to the other, while two wolves (dark buttons), posed as obstacles. This took the strategy of a good shepherd to move his sheep from one pasture to the other. These games, especially "42," were my Mom's favorite pastimes. "42" has also become a favorite between her children and grandchildren. The clicking of dominoes is heard at most family gatherings as the young and the old pair up and have fun speculating, taking risks, and using strategy as they vie to be the ultimate winners. The guys on the team unable to come up with a single win are called skunks. My children could play these games even before they started school.

. . . And then there were eight . . .

Ella was born November 12, 1942, in a year of global turmoil. Pearl Harbor had been devastated by the Japanese in December 1941, and the United States entered World War II. Now the war raged in the Pacific as well as across the Atlantic. War news dominated the radio, the newspapers, conversations on the street corner, and in meetings of neighbors or acquaintances. Just about everyone had someone dear to them in the armed forces.

Ella was baptized Elizabeth Ann, but never went by that name. Her farm name was Ela or Elka; to the outside world she was known as Ella. Even though she is no ones' namesake, she can take comfort that St. Elizabeth, her patron saint, is looking after her. The name Ann came from great-grandmother Anna Betik and grandmother Anna Marusak. I was in the 8th grade the year Ella was born. Ella shares her birth year with Roger Staubach and Barbara Streisand. Mt. Rushmore was being carved in 1942 and Presidents Washington, Jefferson, Teddy Roosevelt, and Lincoln got perched in the Black Hills of South Dakota. In a sporting event, Byron Nelson beat Ben Hogan and won the Master's

Golf Title.

Ella married Bill Heard. Two children were born to them: Shellie and David. Ella and Bill live on a hill in Palmer, Texas, and from her kitchen window she can view the Dallas skyline. This area boasts of having the highest elevation in Ellis County.

1942 continued

In the "Old Country", the entire village of Lidice, Czechoslovakia near Prague, was removed from the face of the earth. The Nazis burned, razed and bulldozed the little village as punishment for the killing of a high-ranking German official, Reinhard Heydrich, called the *Hangman of Europe*. In this reprisal hundreds of men, women, and children were executed. Czechs in America cried. A memorial has been erected to honor those that had been massacred and it stands on the site of Lidice, once a happy little community that is there no more. Some years later, a new little town took root close by and is growing. Prague, the capital of Czechoslovakia, was never bombed by the Germans. They invaded the Czech lands, seized its industries, schools and churches, and crushed its people. Hitler wanted Prague protected because this city had ammunition factories that were vital in supporting his war effort.

The War Years, 1941 to 1945, saw men going off to the service; some enlisted, but most were drafted. Many women also enlisted and served in the military as WACS and WAVES, (US Army and Navy military branches for women). The government set up the Cadet Corp to train more women as nurses. On the home front, women went to work in the defense factories and took jobs vacated by the men gone to the Armed Forces. The people that were left at home planted Victory gardens to ease the shortage of food and cleaned up yards and trash piles and sent all scrap metal to the defense plants. The government issued ration stamps and many commodities were rationed, such as shoes, tires, gasoline, and food such as meat, canned goods, butter, sugar, and many other items. The limit on gasoline was four gallons per week. That's about as much as most people could afford anyway, even at 15 cents per gallon. The Joe Betik family didn't feel the crunch of rationing as much as some families did. Ration stamps were issued according to the number of people in the family. More people, more stamps. We rarely used the stamps for meat, fruits and vegetables because we grew our own. War Bonds were purchased by anyone who had a dollar or two to spare. Patriotism ran deep. Even school kids would forego a treat and put twenty-five cents toward a war bond. The Nuns took charge of this and gave the kids credit toward their bond. Nylon hose were unavailable because the nylon material was needed to make parachutes.

 On sunny days while we were in the fields, the boys in the Army Air Corp. were in the sky practicing to be Ace Pilots. We watched in awe and marveled at the skillful maneuvers as several airplanes in groups nose-dived, flew upside down, spun 'round and 'round and ascended with the greatest of speed. It looked like they were doing a ballet in the sky. They were being trained for air defense against the Germans and the Japanese. Because of its sunny skies, Texas was known to have more flight training days than any other state in the nation. We could watch an air show almost every day. Another consequence of the times was hundreds of ships from different nations were sunk and lost, and the ocean floor must be littered with the wreckage. Most of the losses were attributed to the skillful German torpedo and U-Boats. To prepare for whatever might be ahead, the United States built 488 ships in 1942. In those years, 1941 to 1945, it seemed the American people were more united than any other time in history.

So 1942 was not the best of years. The whole world was in turmoil and my family, like many others, were making do with what there was or doing without. On the farm we were still picking cotton in late November and into December; however, the cotton picking season was nearing the end so we could see light at the end of the tunnel. Ella did not have to spend time in the *buda* like the rest of us did when we were infants. She missed out on the cool breezes wafting through the screened sides.

Life on the farm and "the way it was." Some things just don't change.

Even though this narrative takes us into the 1940's, there are some things not necessarily specific to those times. I mention this here because that's when I began to take notice of some meaningful things. For instance, traditional dishes don't change; a few years or even decades just don't make any difference. Foods like *klobase* (links of specially seasoned smoked sausage), pork roast with dumplings, creamed sauerkraut, chicken noodle soup, desserts of cheese or fruit filled pastry called kolačky, apple strudel, and poppy seed rolls have been around long before my time. These taste bud pleasers and appetite appeasers identify with Czech culture and do any meal proud whether served at weddings, festivals, or Sunday dinner. Here I will tell you how our poppy seed rolls came to be. We called Poppy seed rolls, *makovniky,* and they didn't just happen to be on a platter that we could reach for and enjoy. There was a series of happenings that had to occur before our rolls were made possible. In the spring, Mom's garden always displayed a poppy patch. This was one of Mom's favorite and most pampered projects, but caused her a lot of anxiety. She prayed that the spring storms would not knock down her little poppy crop already three feet tall and full of purple blooms. If there were a lot of thunder and lightening in the post-bloom stage, the pods did not fill out well. If the pods reached maturity and were not gathered in time, the tiny seeds sifted out of the pods. An abundant crop meant many happy little poppy seed rolls. Gathering the poppy seed was a chore. When the blooms fell off and the pod was near being dry, one by one, each pod held upright, was snapped off and dropped in a pillow case or hole-free bucket, then they were spread out to finish drying on a bed sheet on the wagon in the garage. The dry pods were then crushed and removed; trash sifted out and the seed stored. Before it could be used in rolls, the seed was ground in a special little device we called *mlinek* (poppy seed grinder). The ground poppy seed was mixed with sugar, butter, a dab of cornstarch, a hint of lemon, and then used as a filling in the rolls. The wood-burning stove was fired up, rolls made, and put in the oven,

Potatoes by the bushel or by the wagon load

and soon out came the deliciously wonderful pastry. Mom's poppy seed rolls were taken for granted. Neither she, nor the rolls ever received the appreciation they deserved. Today poppy seed can be purchased by the pound or in a can as a ready to use mix. We ate potatoes every day during the week and chicken noodle soup every Sunday. Mom made homemade noodles with eggs from her own hens. If we had more eggs than we could use, the eggs were exchanged for groceries Sunday morning after church. Mom raised a large flock of chickens. She set her own hens and usually one hen could spread herself comfortably over about 18 eggs. The eggs hatched out to baby chicks in three weeks. Occasionally, she ordered straight-run chicks from a hatchery and the mailman delivered them to the house. I think he heard "cheep, cheep" for hours after he completed his route. Pullets were saved for egg layers and the roosters for a dinner. The cocky roosters didn't meet their fate until they were big and chesty and most of the time one was enough for a meal. Smothered fried chicken or chicken rice casserole pleased everyone.

Geese have long been a trade mark of the Czech culture and geese could be seen in most Czech landscapes, especially in the old country. Lyrics were written, pictures painted, and stories told about geese and geese-herders. Farmers raised them to generate a few dollars, but more importantly, for the feathers. When a son or daughter got married, the newlyweds were presented with a goose down featherbed and a set of down feather pillows. Every bed at our home was equipped with a down featherbed and down feather pillows containing feathers from Mom's own geese. We called the feather cover peřina. Mom had her own flock and had special customers for dressed out geese. The customer paid for the goose, Mom kept the feathers. One such customer was a well-to-do lady who had a standing order from year to year. This lady lived in a big house called the Cerf Mansion. In the 1970's, after she had passed away, this big house was dismantled and the present Ennis Public Library stands on this site. It's called the Cerf Library. That big beautiful house should have been restored and preserved. It would have made Ennis proud!

    Mom, as well as neighbors, Mrs. Trpak and Mrs. Krajca, raised turkeys to supplement the farm income. Each household raised about one hundred birds. They roamed freely over the fields picking up grasshoppers and other insects, but eventually the flocks began to mix. All the turkeys looked alike and that made it difficult to reclaim them. To avoid neighborly disputes, each bird owner color-coded her flock. With a stroke of the paint brush over the wing, the turkeys carried their identity wherever they roamed or whichever flock they happen to join. Mom's turkeys wore green, (but St. Patrick had nothing to do with it). Mom sold all the turkeys she raised. I don't recall ever having a roast turkey dinner, not even on Thanksgiving Day. It's not to say we didn't, I just don't remember. However, we did have squab (young pigeons) frequently. To us, it was a special treat. After we had cleaned them, they were quartered and fried, then smothered in gravy. The aroma filled the house and drifted outside, and we could hardly wait for the dinner call. The smaller kids piled behind the table and sat against the wall on a homemade bench the length of the dinner table. If we happened to be chewing gum (which was rare), we saved it by sticking it on the window frame behind us, or under the ledge of the table. It was retrieved later, dipped in the sugar bowl and enjoyed all over again. At mealtime we crumbled homemade bread on our plate and sopped it with the gravy. Our family surrounded the dinner table and there were many plates to fill but there were always enough squabs to go around, even for seconds. Daddy made pigeon hotels and attached them to the side of the barn out of reach of predators, like our cats. We had to prop a ladder when we made the routine hotel room check. Checkout time was when the squab were nearly grown.

    Besides turkeys, geese, and chickens running around in the yard, a few guineas could be seen flitting around amongst them. The guineas took care of themselves. Usually they laid their eggs in the Johnson grass, and hatched them out on their own. We'd see them when they brought their little brood home; the baby guineas were quick as lightening. At night most of the guineas would roost up in the trees around the house and watched everything going on around them. They made lots of noise when things were not right. Not only were they good watchdogs, but they also made a pot of wonderful noodle soup if you could catch one.

    Milking the cows was a regular chore that couldn't be put off. We milked twice a day, rain or shine; in the morning before going to school and in the evening at sundown. The art of milking is a developed skill, and you can get good finger and hand exercises, better than squeezing a physical therapy ball. Usually we had company, because our cats waited for us at the barn. They sat nearby as we milked and just waited for a stream of milk to be directed at them. They lapped it up like pros, scarcely losing a drop. We had some happy cats. Each cow had a name and we had our favorites to milk. Most of the time the cows were quite gentle, except when they were bothered by horseflies. The tail would swish from one side to the other and frequently we got whacked over the head with it. It wasn't too bad unless the tail was loaded with cockle burs and it got hung in our hair. And we were always alert for the unexpected side kick too. We did not use a milking stool like a lot of milkers did because it was just in the way if we had to make a quick jump. The milk was strained into large stoneware bowls, each holding one to two gallons of milk, then covered with cheese cloth and placed on a table on the back porch. In a matter of few hours, the sweet cream rose to the top and it was easy to scoop off. After a few skims, there was enough cream to make butter. In the spring when the pastures were green and lush, the milk was richer and there was a heavier layer of cream that rose to the top of the milk. Not being refrigerated, the milk soon soured and by the next day it had already turned to clabber. Mom made cheese out of the clabber, but she'd save some for Daddy because he liked to drink it like buttermilk. Our breakfast cereal, oatmeal, Cream of Wheat, or cornmeal mush with pieces of bacon, was cooked with milk. My favorite was the Cream of Wheat with cinnamon and sugar. Our cows provided good wholesome milk, but sometimes in the spring, the taste was altered when the cows grazed where wild onions were mixed with the grass. We drank onion-flavored milk. In the summer, the pastures were burnt up from the heat and lack of rain and the only viable grass in the pasture was the broom weed. The broom weed gave the milk a bitter twang. We drank it anyway, but not as much.

    The sweet cream made a delicate and wonderful treat when spread on a slice of hot bread fresh from the oven and sprinkled with sugar and cinnamon; or sweet cream mixed with jam or jelly and spread over the fresh bread. It was so yummy that just thinking about it, we could scarcely wait to get home from school. Each of us did our own variation from a recipe that was so simple, but the treat so divine. We ate it on the way to the field. When we got home from school each day, we went to work in the field until dark. Another sweet cream "best" was to scoop the cream off the milk and spread it generously over hot new potatoes, add a little salt and pepper and enjoy! We never grew tired of it even though we had many a meal of potatoes and cream only. A milk truck came by on schedule and collected milk from farmers who had surplus milk to sell. We didn't sell milk, because we utilized all we had; but I think the Trojaceks sold their surplus. They milked many cows, and often while we were still working in the fields, we watched the Trojaceks, (Anton, Leslie, Jerry, and Adolf), as they walked the road to the hill to feed the cattle and milk the cows. We couldn't understand how they could be through for the day, and be home from the field, when there were still at least two more hours of sunlight left.

In his quiet way, Daddy exercised his skills and talents and did things not common to everyone, such as making his whiskey or brewing his own beer; not to sell, but to treat friends and neighbors when they came over. He had a good product, and anyone who was offered a drink felt like a "Very Important Person." This brings to my mind how we viewed one local man who loved a good sip, and came by frequently on the pretense of buying cattle. He was a cattleman and a meat processor. We knew he always liked to have a chaser after he had downed his whiskey, so one day we deliberately left the water bucket dry. He was ranting all the while he was drawing up some water from the well. We thought it was funny and snickered, but stayed out of sight. When the neighbors came over to help Daddy with a difficult task or just to visit, Daddy always treated them to a *šluk* (jiggerful).

While Daddy enjoyed making his whiskey and beer, Mom was making Root Beer. We had helped her make it so many times we knew exactly what to do. In a ten-gallon stoneware crock we'd pour five gallons of lukewarm water, one packet of yeast, five pounds of sugar, and two ounces of root beer extract, then stirred it until it was all dissolved and well blended. Clean, recycled beer bottles, a box of new bottle caps, and bottle capper were all on hand to finish this project. When the bottles were filled and capped, they were laid on their side and placed in the cool cellar for two or three days. We knew it was ready when we would hear a bottle explode.

Daddy also had a hobby of collecting coins. He had many Indian Head pennies, Buffalo nickels, and other coins from the 1800's. He was proud of his collection and kept it in the cellar where he felt it was safe. After Daddy passed away, one of his ten kids claimed it.

Daddy was a patient man and slow to anger, but there were a few times when he just got fed up. As mentioned before, my father did not like to be pushed by anyone. This brings to my mind the time Daddy was driving along down the old Highway 75, which at that time was a winding, hilly, single lane highway too treacherous to do any passing. (In the 1960's, Hwy. 75 was restructured as I-45). An impatient female was tailgating very closely and honking her horn, wanting Daddy to speed up. Finally he pulled off the road and let her pass, then he said, "Babo, když chteš jed, toš jedem!" If he had said it in English, it would have sounded like this: "Old Hag, if you vont to go, vee go!" He stayed on her tail and gave her a good run in her jalopy. We had many a good laugh over this incident, but mostly because complaisant Daddy had enough and lost his cool. Could this be called Road Rage?

CHAPTER X
THE FOUR SEASONS OF THE YEAR
- COUNTRY STYLE

Seasonal color and seasonal spice made everything so nice. All the seasons express the times in their own colorful way, and each one offers seasonal spice and flavor to our reflections and musings of the days gone by. There were pleasures and perils associated with each of the changing times. On the farm an unsuspected and unexpected disaster could loom up from anywhere on any day. How did we grow up to adulthood? And how did Mom and Dad keep their sanity midst all the nonsensical things we did?

Downhill Roll

When I think of the seasons, I

see each one like a spoke in a wheel and the rim that forms the circle never disconnects. The timing of each season overlaps and blends with the other. Sometimes it's hard to tell where one stops and the other begin, yet each season has a distinctive character of its own. Nowhere in the world is it more clearly defined and visible as on the farm. We associated summer with endless number of days in the fields, sun up to sun down. The days were long, hot, and dry. This time of the year has always been my least favorite, but we had many good times and I have many pleasant memories just the same. Summer heat came from the same source then as it does today, but we had no air-conditioning or fans to escape from it. Sometimes the heat got so stifling and oppressive we'd go outside at night to sleep, hoping for a breeze. We climbed up to the top of the wagon full of cotton (ready to go to the gin in the morning), and laid there gazing at the stars. We could identify the constellations, the Big Dipper, the Little Dipper, and have fun doing our own little creations with the clumping of the stars. Out in the country, without competition from guard lights, porch lights, and city lights, the stars in the heavens were seen in infinite numbers and were bigger and brighter than anyone could imagine. The bright and smiling moon seemed to be saying "Everything is under control."

We entertained ourselves whether we were doing late chores at night, checking the trot lines with Daddy as we walked along the river bank, or by rolling tires down the road with the neighbor's kids. Fireflies were in such abundance. Looking around us it seemed the heavens had dropped down and the horizon disappeared as the myriad of stars just blended in with the twinkling fireflies all around us. There were hundreds of fire flies transforming our surroundings into a Fairyland. They added mystic, magic, and a romantic fantasy to a dark or a moonlit night!

Mosquitoes were bigger, braver, and more of them, or so it seemed. Chiggers, this "C-Word," was synonymous with summer. It didn't matter if we were baling hay, picking cotton, or just fishing, the tiny little microscopic boogers found their host and migrated to their favorite places, like the waist band or under the arms. Most folks were allergic to the chigger bites, some more, some less, leaving an irritation on the skin that seemed to itch forever. The best way to get rid of the chiggers was to anoint them with a mixture of goose grease, sulfur and kerosene. After "the kill," the allergic reaction remained for several days but the inflammation could be eased by applying *Kafrova Mast* (Watkin's salve). It's astounding how much misery can be caused by the bite of a tiny mite.

When evening came at the end of a hot summer day, the sun had set and the day's work was done, we felt dusty, grimy, tired, and sweaty. A swim in the stock pond was as refreshing as a rejuvenating tonic. Many times the neighbor kids joined us and we stayed in the water a long time, sometimes in total darkness when the moon was not out, and never counted heads!

Oh, the pleasures and perils of country living! It

didn't bother us kids one bit to aggravate Dad's angry bull out in the open pasture. His head down low to the ground, his front hoofs clawing the dirt, and all the while snorting and making those awful sounds as his glaring eyes watched us crawling towards him on all fours, mimicking him and booing him. There was not a tree or a fence close-by. If he had charged us, he could have torn us up. I can only surmise our Guardian Angel must have put a restraining hand on him.

We explored the Trinity River when it went out of banks after heavy rains. Daddy and the neighbors, Mr. Krajca and Mr. Trpak, would go there and ford the currents and often catch the fish in the ebbing waters. Sometimes they took us and the neighbor's kids along. The water was flowing rapidly and was well above our knees, so we tucked our skirts up and treaded through the water barefoot. We were lucky none of us were swept downstream with the current. Snakes? They never crossed our minds and we never saw them cross our paths.

Mary Betik Trojacek

The days in the field were Same-O, Same-O, day after day, but were punctuated with a few diversions. We knew how many buzzards there were flying overhead and we were amused by the killdeer faking a broken wing and fussing just to keep us from nearing her nest somewhere on our row. We encountered an occasional snake slithering in front of us and we'd tease it with our hoe 'til it spit foam. The Black Widow spider always built her home by the same blueprint so it was easy to identify; most often she could be found on a corn stalk, her web wrapped around a dry husk of corn. We were wary of her when we were pulling corn. Every once in a while, a centipede (*Sto Noha,* meaning 100-legged), emerged from a crack in the parched ground. The shiny eight to ten inch long, blue-black centipede with bright orange legs was said to be poisonous. It was easy to spot and we avoided it, but didn't feel threatened by it. It usually headed for the nearest crack in the ground and disappeared as fast as its one hundred legs could move. We found the big yellow and black spider a source of entertainment too. His web usually spanned the aisle between the cotton rows and he was positioned in the middle, waiting for an unwary insect to fly into his web-trap. The activity of the spider fascinated us as we threw moths, loopers, and grasshoppers into his net. But another side to the drama of the spider was, when we were bent over, busy, and intent on picking cotton, our peripheral vision obscured with a bonnet, we would run into this web head first. Then woe is me, we frantically searched for the spider among the cotton leaves on the stalk. If we saw it on the stalk, we knew the spider had not stayed behind our collar. Big red ants (about one half inch long) were quite common in the fields and pastures. Some mounds measured 36" across, but we rarely see them now. Horned toads and tarantulas seemed to have met their demise too.

Some folks could tell the time of day by the length of

a shadow cast, but we knew it was 4:00 p.m. when we heard the drone of the airplane and saw it reflecting in the western sky as it made its daily flight, probably from San Antonio to Dallas. As we stood there barefoot, leaning on our hoe, our right foot resting on our left knee, and bonnet pulled back, we scanned the skies and watched the fluffy white clouds

"Please let it rain! Please let it rain!"

slowly change shape. Even though we could tell there was not a hint of rain in them, we said a silent prayer of reprieve just the same. Money was always on the short side, and when an opportunity came up to earn a little extra, we took advantage of it. Mom and Dad let us keep whatever we earned. The more cotton we picked, the greater the pay. We picked cotton for other folks who needed help, mostly neighbors and relatives. I remember how amazed this one neighbor, Mr. Ed Slovacek was when he saw that I could pick 350 pounds of cotton in a day. That's picking, not pulling. I was 12 or 13 years old at the time. Looking back, I'm inclined to marvel at myself too! The field where we picked cotton for Uncle Louis Marusak in Bardwell can now be called a "once-upon-a-time-cotton-patch," because that area is under water, consumed by Lake Bardwell, and the landscape of Uncle Louis's farm will never be the same.

We did not get an allowance as such, but Mom and Dad always paid us at the end of summer; enough for us to buy school clothes and school supplies, and still have a little left over. After they purchased the additional acreage from Mr. O'Quinn, Daddy gave us a three acre patch of bottom land; the proceeds of which we kids could keep. We kept track of how much each one picked, and then were paid accordingly. Usually, our patch yielded about two bales of cotton. We felt rich! Mom and Dad imposed no conditions on how to spend the money left over after we bought our necessities. Thinking back now, I can't believe I bought a pair of spiked high-heel shoes, and what's even harder to believe is that I wore them to church! And after one other shopping spree, I came home with a wide brim southern-belle type hat. I wore it to church too.

Throughout the 1940's we had picked cotton with all of our cousins at one time or another; all except the Kosareks. But every summer the Kosarek boys came over and helped Daddy bale hay. Recalling those days, I can see how hard it must have been for Daddy to get set up for hay baling. Daddy cut the hay, with a mule team, and then allowed it to dry for a couple of days. Then it was ready to be raked with a mule-team-rake (Lillie did a lot of this), and little hay stacks were made using a pitch-fork. When it was time to bale the hay, these little hay stacks were delivered to the press with a buck rake and mule team. In those days the hay baler was called a "press." The press was made stationary. The team of mules hitched to the press, went around and around and around, setting the press in motion, causing the jack to go up and down pressing the hay into bales. One guy took his place at the side of the press and with his pitch fork, kept the table supplied with hay, while another guy stood on top of the table and with his pitch fork, fed the press. This guy had the most hazardous job. He had to be very careful not to slip and fall into the "mouth" as he was filling the press with hay. The hay baling crew was not complete if there was not someone to tie the bales; two were needed, and usually one of the Kosarek boys and one of us girls, Helen, Lillie, Mildred or I, sat on opposite sides of the press. Using baling wire, we tied the hay into bales. One punched the wire through to the other side, and the other guy punched it back. It was tied as the bale progressed toward the finish line. The size of the bale depended on these two guys. At a given time, one of us would holler "B...L...O...C...K," and the guy feeding the press would drop a wooden block into the hole. This kept the bales separated, but we had to make sure we didn't tie the block to the bale. The last of the crew was the puller and the stacker who pulled the finished bales out of the way and stacked them into a neat square pile. As technology improved, the tractor replaced the mules, and the press was set in motion using a long wide belt connecting the press to the tractor. An even more impressive change came a few years later.

We baled all day in the heat and dust, and then at twilight we welcomed a swim in the stock tank. The Kosarek boys and we made a good work team and turned work into fun. Mother cooked for the workers and always prepared a nice meal. As the years went by, her pineapple cream pies were still remembered. The bales of hay, arranged neatly in square stacks, still waited to be hauled off and stored in the barn the next day. To me, this job was not one to fight over, and did not require much education. It could be had by anyone with a strong back, strong arms, a hay hook, and a sweat rag. Baling hay in those days was a major project for the farmer. He could manage the necessary preparations alone, but for the hay baling he had to have a crew, so he scouted for help days in advance. Today hay baling has been reduced to a one-man operation. This "one-man crew" sits in an air-conditioned tractor cab, pushing buttons or pulling levers, and listening to his favorite music on the radio, while the *"press"* spits out the bales.

Meals on Wheels

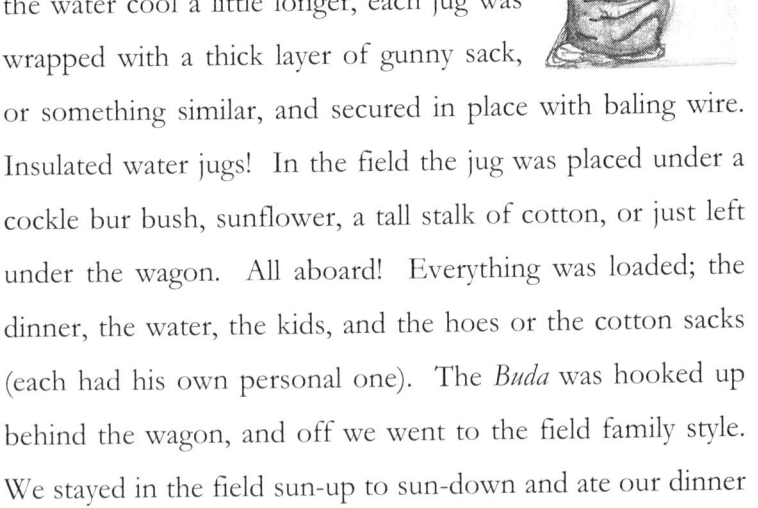

Time was of the essence in peak cotton season and many times we took our dinner to the field to save "traveling time" to the house at noon. We planned to stay in the field all day, so the dinner was prepared early in the morning. The water jugs were filled with cool water from the well. In order to keep the water cool a little longer, each jug was wrapped with a thick layer of gunny sack, or something similar, and secured in place with baling wire. Insulated water jugs! In the field the jug was placed under a cockle bur bush, sunflower, a tall stalk of cotton, or just left under the wagon. All aboard! Everything was loaded; the dinner, the water, the kids, and the hoes or the cotton sacks (each had his own personal one). The *Buda* was hooked up behind the wagon, and off we went to the field family style. We stayed in the field sun-up to sun-down and ate our dinner under the wagon or in the shade of a nearby tree. Today this could be called an all day summer picnic with Meals on Wheels. Some of our favorite dinners were chicken and rice casserole, chicken in corn meal dressing, and rice pudding with lots of raisins. Leftover breakfast pancakes sprinkled with cinnamon and sugar, and rolled like a burrito, made a delightful snack. The water in our insulated jug did not stay cool very long and soon we were drinking warm water.

Mom made us wear sun bonnets and jumpers (long sleeved shirt), and long pants in the field. It was important that young girls strive to be fair young ladies. Some years later the younger generation discarded this protection as they went to fields wearing midriffs and shorts, hatless and shoeless, in an attempt to get a good suntan like their city peers who were laying out in the sun getting tanned.

We learned cooking skills from Mom, but many times we just experimented when Mom sent us home early to prepare a meal. Some of these original recipes did not suit everyone's fancy and some gripes and complaints were kicked around, but it seemed there never were any leftovers.

We had a large vegetable garden close to the house. Here we grew onions, tomatoes, lettuce, and other vegetables and were easily accessible when meals were prepared quickly. We also had a garden plot in the bottom field and there we planted cantaloupes, watermelons and cucumbers in larger tracts. It seemed the cantaloupes, and watermelons all ripened at the same time and there were more than we could eat, so we hauled them by the wagon load and fed them to the hogs and chickens. Before we threw the watermelon over the fence, we cracked it open and ate the sweet, seedless center. We gathered cucumbers by the bushel basket, washed them in a #3 galvanized tub, and then processed them into jars for pickles. Mom's dill pickles always had a generous amount of dill in the jar which made them so good. Every year the dill came up on its own and we had dill growing everywhere.

The Apron

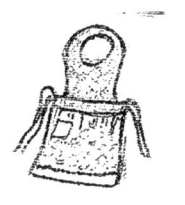

The apron was as essential to the Lady of the House as baling wire was to the Man of the Land. Each had many uses.... a multi-purpose creation or tool. Usually the apron was an "original copy", made of a scrap of material or flour sack not large enough to make a dress. Some were plain and some were made fancy by adding rick-rack, or ruffles. Every Mom or Auntie had one or two easily accessible at the kitchen entrance hanging on a nail by the door or by the kitchen stove. It served as a handy pot-holder while cooking dinner or when adding firewood to an already hot stove or heater, or when pulling a pan of hot strudel out of the oven. It also served as a protective garment. Her dress underneath the apron was kept free of stains and smudges, especially the tummy area. When unexpected company came, the lady shed the apron, dried her hands on and she was quickly transformed to a gracious hostess welcoming her guests. The apron turned into an instant basket upon finding eggs in the barn by chance or it was a catch-all for baby chicks frantically running around the chicken coop before a storm. The lady might go to the garden for an onion and return with cukes and tomatoes too, all gathered up in her apron. The apron was like an attached hand towel. Hands were dried quickly as she headed to tend to a little one. Many teary eyes, runny noses, drooling mouths or bruised knees were lovingly dabbed with the apron.

Today an apron is more of a novelty not used very often by the Lady of the House. Who needs one anyway, when all she has to do is reach into the deep-freeze for a TV dinner and pop it into the microwave oven?

The Baling Wire ...

The baling wire fixed anything and everything. The Man of the Land did not have to have a degree to be called a Southern Engineer. He acquired his engineering skills through necessity and hands-on experience. This multi-purpose tool was free because it was recycled and always readily available hanging in large circular clusters on fence posts around the barn. Fences were repaired, gates were hung, and gates were held closed with a loop of baling wire. It held in place the insulation on water jugs (a wet tote sack). The distal corner of the cotton sack with a loop made of baling wire provided the means for weighing cotton. Toys were fixed, mufflers secured, and in the forties, some farmers spliced and stretched it to keep the cows in the pasture with the electric fence. The baling wire served as a quick fix if a hammer and nail was not on hand. I've even seen trousers held up with baling wire. So you can see why the baling wire was highly respected. Today, most folks don't have baling wire on hand and instead of fixing things, they just discard it.

Farm Labor standing on the street corner

Mary Betik Trojacek

Local or migrant folks wanting to work in the fields usually gathered on a street corner where a farmer in need of temporary help could go and pick up as many as he needed. This type of arrangement helped the farmer and the people in need of work had a chance to earn a few dollars. Agricultural technology was changing and improving rapidly. We can see a good example of this as we look at the mechanics of harvesting cotton. First we used to pick cotton, and then the gins improved and did a better job of cleaning trash out of the cotton, so we began to pull cotton, and then along came the cotton stripper. By the late 1940's, most of the cotton was harvested with the cotton stripper. The early models did not do a very good job, so we kids had to take our cotton sacks and go scrapping, and pick up all the cotton that the stripper missed, lost, and left behind. The cotton stripper took away a lot of the summer stress. What the farmers liked best about the cotton stripper was that usually by the end of September the cotton harvest was near completion. Years ago, we were still picking cotton around Christmas time. Agriculture technology continued to advance rapidly and just when the farmer could take advantage of the improved machinery and herbicides and farming became less stressful on the body, the "smart generation" found easier ways to make a living. They abandoned the cotton land and put it all in pasture, then got a job in the city. As a result, we no longer see groups of people standing on the street corner waiting to be picked up so they could work in the fields and make a few dollars. The smart generation and modern technology had reduced the demand for them to zero; but on the other hand, even if field work was available, I doubt that we would see very many people knocked down because they had been trying to beat someone else to a job in the fields! There is no further need for tons of duck cloth yardage that had gone into making cotton sacks. Someone in the cotton mill lost his job.

Making haystacks with Daddy

There were some tasks on the farm that were too difficult for Daddy to do alone, so who else was there, but one of us girls to help him? The boys were not big enough yet. One such job that demanded a helping hand was building haystacks. Daddy and I made many haystacks together. This was extra feed for the cattle and the storing of hay this way required the labor of only two people. We hauled the dry hay by the wagon loads, and began building haystacks close to the barn.

Making Hay Stacks with Daddy

With a pitchfork, Daddy would toss the hay in my direction, and I would grab it with my pitch fork and distribute it evenly so we would have a balanced stack. Higher and higher the stack grew, until Daddy was not able to pitch the hay any higher. All done, the only way down, was for me to slide down. I threw the pitchfork way off to the side and down I went. Daddy and I made a fine team and I enjoyed building haystacks with him, even though it was a hot and dusty job and there were more fun ways to spend the summer. There were other jobs on the farm that would have been more fitting for boys, but Mom and Dad only had four girls at first, so we, especially Lillie, always had a job. Lillie worked the field with Rubik and Rudik many times to help Daddy.

Pulling corn.

Harvesting corn was a team effort (the mules and us). Rubik and Rudik pulled the wagon. They had wire baskets over their mouths to keep them from ruining the corn as they went down the corn rows. We took a swat of several rows, broke the dry ears of corn off the stalks and threw them in the wagon. The one who ran the row next to the wagon didn't need a very strong arm, but he had the hardest job of all because he had to pick up all the ears that were thrown too short or overthrown and missed the wagon. The one next to the wagon was also a target for a hit, especially if there was an unsettled score. The guys in the farthest rows could have used some baseball skills. The team-mate who had the most enviable job of all was the one on the wagon. With reins in hand, he motioned the mules with a "giddy-up" and the mules moved forward; then a with little pull on the reins and a "whoa," they came to a stop. The one on the wagon also had the duty to observe where the overthrown ears of corn had landed and direct the retriever to them. The corn stalk with the Black Widow spider was left for the crows.

Summers were highlighted with the 4th of July dance, the Feast of the Assumption Celebration on August 15th, and the Church Bazaar at summer's end.

Mary Betik Trojacek

Summer takes a bow and slowly eases out as Autumn is ushered in.

Oh, the nostalgia of autumn! So many of my memories are linked to this special time of the year. Autumn takes me back in time to the cotton fields, where we could see the sky meet the horizon with very little clutter. As we scanned the skies, often we could see flocks of ducks or geese flying south in a "V" formation; the honkers and the quackers could be heard even before they were seen. Nowhere else could we view them better than from these wide-open spaces. With the demise of the cotton patch, it seems there are fewer and fewer of these graceful birds making their annual flight to their winter refuge, or do we not see as many because we are too busy, and too distracted by noises of traffic, television, the telephone, and other intrusions? In recent years, I have not had the pleasure of seeing very many flocks as they made their way south. I miss the honkers and the quackers!

In later autumn and before the first killing frost, often we would come across a lone tomato bush just loaded with juicy red cherry tomatoes as we gathered the last remnants of the cotton crop. What a treat! Those were the best tomatoes we ever ate. Sometimes we'd find a volunteer cantaloupe or watermelon vine on our row that had withstood the heat of the summer and recuperated in the early fall. A little surprise clinging to the vine was not always perfect, but how sweet it was! Pleasures left over from summer.

As the brisk north wind blows and the Autumn leaves fall and the trees become bare, I watch the leaves roll, rustle, and dance across my yard and the scene suggests to me that pecans too must be falling, so with a bucket in one hand and a stick in the other I soon find myself poking among leaves and dry summer-spent grass. While I'm picking up the little gems, I recall the pecan picking ventures of the past when Mom, Dad, and the kids, all went to the woods to gather pecans. As Daddy trashed the trees, we picked up the fallen nuts. They were not very big, nor were they paper shell, but they were pecans. As my mind drifts into the past, I'm thinking that Autumn shouldn't pass one by, without giving the pleasure of gathering a bounty of pecans, while taking this quiet time to daydream, think things out, meditate, or pray. As I reminisce, I'm inclined to believe that we receive double pleasure from God's freebies. First from picking the pecans, either in solitude or on a pecan-picking picnic, then later eating cakes and strudels just chock-full of the tasty nuts . . . just like Mom used to make.

    After the first frost the Autumn Hags came out. We could see them floating about in the air, get hung on the fence or a tree branch, or clinging to a frostbitten blade of Johnson grass. Some would fly by us with the speed of the wind and we'd try to knock them down. In the year of an early frost, they showed up quite appropriately around Halloween. In Czech, we called them *Podzimny Babi*. Autumn Hags were long strands of cobwebs that the wind had loosened off brush and grasses and the sight of them heralded in the fall season. It takes the wide-open spaces like the cotton patch to be entertained by something as simple as the Autumn Hags.

    Halloween came in October, but for all we knew it could have come in April, since we didn't go Trick or Treat, but we did associate Halloween with pumpkins and Jack-o-lanterns. Growing up on the farm, kids didn't get into trouble; they were kept busy, so they didn't have time for too much mischief. However, some of them did grow a wild hair or two. When Halloween came around, they exercised their ingenious ideas and played tricks on people with the confidence that their actions would be taken as something that was to be expected since it was Halloween. One of the old time favorite pranks played in the days gone by, and continued to be played in my day, was to flip over the outhouse of the intended dupe. This was a good way to get even with someone without repercussion. Anyone who had an idea of being a potential victim was alert and wary on Halloween night, and went to the privy with caution, because they didn't know if they were on the "S list" . . . meaning select list, of course.

The Harvest Dance *(Vino Brani)* was an occasion to celebrate a bountiful fall harvest. The hall was decorated with a harvest theme and corn, grapes, and other items related to harvest, were strung up and hanging from the ceiling, but barely reachable. There were several lodge members appointed as "policemen" to maintain order and encourage thievery. While the people were dancing, the "policemen" were watching everyone. They were ever alert to catch a thief. Anyone caught stealing any of the harvest had to pay a hefty fine. This was a fun way of increasing the coffers of the hall. I don't think it generated much money because the "criminals" usually outsmarted the "lawmen" and made a getaway, or just passed the loot to someone else.

Getting firewood ready for the cold winter was a big job for Daddy to do alone and often a little bit of help was a big help. After the fall crops had been harvested, Daddy and I, Rubik and Rudik, and Dad's dogs, went to the woods and made firewood. Daddy cut the tree down with an ax, and then we used a push-pull saw, about a six-footer with a handle on each end. Daddy on one end and I on the other . . . push-pull, push-pull we sawed the trees into manageable logs. Enough firewood was made so the heater would continue to provide us with heat, and the kitchen stove to continue to cook our meals for months to come. We spent the whole day in the woods. It was so peaceful there; the serenity interrupted only by the echoes of a wood-choppers axe, the birds in the trees, an occasional flock of geese, and the rustle of falling leaves. Daddy's dogs had a good time snooping around in the brush. Soon we would hear their excited yapping as they flushed out a rabbit. If they caught it, they'd bring it back to Daddy. It seems we never went home without a rabbit or two.

Autumn was my favorite time of the year and I often wished it would last longer than it did, but as the days dwindled on toward winter, we let go of autumn, and began to think of what winter might have in store for us. This was the time when life on the farm went into slow gear. We could look forward to reading many library books, fact or fiction; it didn't matter. They offered adventure and fantasy. We could hike through the woods, explore the creek bed, and pick up any little treasures that had drifted in during heavy rains. We could take swinging leaps across the creek bed on an old possum grape vine hanging down from a tree high above us (we were the undiscovered Tarzans). We could look around and see what was left over from summer and autumn.

Winter time was hog-killing time, sewing and quilting time, corn shucking time, and feather-stripping time. It was wood cutting time, trapping and hunting time.

.............And Christmas was nigh……..

We often ate fried sweet potatoes, sauerkraut soup, and whatever Daddy brought home from his hunt. Stripping feathers was for the birds, and we didn't look forward to that very much. The feather stripping took place in the winter time around a wood-burning heater. It was not a good idea to strip feathers in the summer . . . no air conditioning, and breezes from an open window were not allowed because the fine down would float away in the air. Also, the feather-stripper perspired and the fine down stuck to his skin. So stripping feathers in the winter time worked out best, but it had one disadvantage. Usually there was one stripper who had the sneezes and the coughs. Feathers flew! This stripper was looking for an excuse, but usually the ploy didn't work.

Feather-stripping scenario.

Just imagine yourself being a feather stripper sitting by a cozy fire. There are a few other strippers so you don't feel alone. It's like a feather-stripping bee with light hearted and idle chatter going on. Next to your chair is this big sack, stuffed full with feathers. One by one, the fluffy down is stripped off the quill. (If the quills are not removed, they will come out through the pillow and poke you when you lay your head down.) It takes a long time to make a dent in the sack. Do you know how many feathers there are in a sack full of feathers? I don't either. These feathers were those plucked and collected from the many geese Mom cleaned and sold. She made featherbeds and pillows for our beds and some to give away as gifts. Some years later the loud-speaking radio rescued us from boredom. We rarely missed listening to the *Hill Billy Hit Parade*, which came on right after the 10:00 p.m. news. The comedy *Amos and Andy* was Daddy's favorite. We listened to *The Lone Ranger, Inner Sanctum, Life of Riley*, and many others, but we never got involved with the "soaps," even though everyone had become acquainted with *Helen Trent* by this time. Helen Trent was the star in one of the earliest of soap operas on the radio. The soaps were known by everyone as "stories" and had a wide following. We had no doubt that *Minnie Pearl* was alive and well and enjoying the height of her popularity as we listened to the *Grand Old Opry*.

During the winter months the chicken house and the barn stalls were cleaned out. The manure was loaded on a wagon and hauled out, then scattered over the garden plot, the blackberry patch and in the orchard. In those days, that was the most common fertilizer known to the farmer. And it was cheap and readily available.

Corn shucking was saved for cold or rainy days. Daddy liked to have the corn shucked in advance because it saved on feeding time. Sometimes we spent the entire day in the barn and the pile of shucked corn grew and got bigger and bigger, and as we shucked, we counted those yellow ears of corn. (To this day, I don't know why we counted them.) The corn crib was a haven (or heaven) for mice. Our cats were always on stand-by for a Happy Meal. The mountain of corn shucks was kicked out and put in the manger for the cows to eat

Winter time made us wish for snow and snow ice cream!

Mardi Gras was referred to as Masquerade Ball by many folks, but we called it *Maśkarni Bal*. This was once a popular event in our little town and it was held the weekend before Ash Wednesday. The young people dressed in original costumes and their disguise was the talk of the ball. Everyone was speculating on who was behind the mask. This was the last fun time before Lent began. Lent was time for penance, soul searching, and giving up pleasures like dances, parties, weddings, candy and other sweet treats, and entertainment.

In late winter, Mom started her hot bed outside on the south and sunny side of the house. She planted cabbage, kohl-rabi, tomato and other vegetable seeds, then covered the frame with a large window pane to permit the sun to warm her little seedlings. This was her mini hot house and the plants were ready for transplanting when the danger of frost was over. It gave her satisfaction to have the first cucumbers and ripe tomatoes on Mother's Day.

Then it seemed we just blinked our eyes and Spring had sprung!

We had survived the cold winter and all of a sudden it was Spring. The Redbuds and the fruit trees burst out in bloom and the sweet fragrance of the plum blossoms permeated the air all over the farm. The Lilac bushes and the Chinaberry trees bloomed in delicate shades of purple and had the most pleasant fragrance. Mom's Jonquils, Pansies, and Petunias added scent and scenery to the landscape around the house, while the Bluebonnets and the Indian Paintbrushes captured the spotlight on the hills. The pastures flushed out in green and gave contentment to Daddy's cows; his honey bees were humming and were busy doing what they did best.

It was time to ventilate the house, to get rid of all the smoke and kerosene odors which had accumulated during the winter. We opened the doors and windows and let the fresh spring air flow through the house and the lacy curtains waved about in the breeze. Today a sense of nostalgia comes over me whenever I see such a scene. The young generation raised in airtight homes with A.C. will rarely experience the good feeling that comes from cool, calming, refreshing breezes coming through open windows and watching the curtains leisurely flap and wave around in the breeze. Floors mopped with pine-oil dried quickly. We freshened featherbeds, quilts, and pillows by draping them over the garden fence and let them bask in the sun and fresh air.

Some of the vegetables in the garden were at their prime and ready to compliment a meal. The English peas seemed to be saying "pick me," so we obeyed and just sat down on the row, picked the peas off the vine, cracked the pod, placed it between our teeth, and stripped the peas out. We chewed the pea pod till all the juice and flavor was gone. Usually there was a telltale little pile of cud where we had sat and enjoyed a helping of the freshest of vegetables found anywhere. We checked out the turnip row too and knew which one was best. We pulled it up, knocked the dirt off, gave it a few good strokes against the side of our pants, then holding it by the root we peeled it with our teeth and enjoyed our treat.

And we could tell that spring had sprung, when the Robins and the Meadow Larks were singing and doing their hop; the sparrows were building nests and Mom was setting hens on eggs for baby chicks to hatch while Dad was proudly counting his baby calves when they "dropped."

Easter was approaching and Mom made sure each one of us had a new Easter dress. In anticipation of Easter, many fashion-minded gals were wishing for some magic to ward off or delay any cold snap headed our way, so that there would be no need to wear a coat. On Easter Sunday the church was a dazzling picture of color and fashion with new hats, new shoes, and new dresses. All the girls and women dressed in their best and their finest. This is not intended to misconstrue the image and general intentions of the ladies, because as a whole they were good Christians and prayed regularly. Most of the girls and ladies didn't get a new dress anytime they had a whim for one. New outfits were had for special occasions and Easter was one of them. At this special time they had the personal satisfaction of letting the world know they dressed in their finest to honor the Risen Christ.

Mom's Flower Garden - For therein amongst her flowers, her pleasures lie.

Mom derived much pleasure from the simple things in life. To see her flower garden in bloom in an array of many colors was one of her greatest joys. Her garden was a mix of perennials, annuals, and volunteers. If a pansy or a petunia came up in the onion row, that's where it stayed. The happy faces of the Johnny Jump Ups, the bright orange hue of the Cosmos, the sweet fragrance of the old fashion Petunia or Sweet Williams, gave quiet pleasure to her heart and peace and tranquility to her soul. Spring wouldn't be spring in Mom's garden without the Larkspur, (in Czech they were called *Kozy Bradi,* "goat's chin"). These volunteers bloomed on spikes in colors of dark blue, pink, and white. We made delicate little wreaths out of them and pressed them to dry. The Hollyhocks, standing tall and proud by the garden gate seemed to be saying "welcome" to anyone passing through. And one could always find an antique rose in bloom, large, pink, full of grace, beautiful and fragrant. When the petals fell off, we often found a round pod that remained on the stem. Finders, keepers; keepers, eaters. Was that Rose hips we were eating?

    Mom's flowers went to church too. Mom made little baskets for us and proudly filled them with her flowers and sprigs of the feathered out asparagus. They added glory to special church celebrations, like Christ the King procession, May Crowning, or on Holy Saturday. All the little girls dressed in white, and carrying little baskets of sweet-scented petals walked in a procession ahead of the Blessed Sacrament, dropping the petals to enhance and beautify the path of the Lord.

Mary Betik Trojacek

Making sauerkraut

In our big vegetable garden, we grew the simple vegetables like green beans, oak leaf lettuce, cucumbers, potatoes, garlic, onion, tomatoes, and cabbage. There were always the intention and hope of surpluses for canning and storing. Cabbage, we grew a plenty. When the cabbage heads were big and round and plump they were ready to be cut out. A day was set aside just for making sauerkraut. The large heads were trimmed, wedged, and shredded. We would have two or three wash-tubs full of shredded cabbage on the back porch or under a tree. The kids were told to scrub their feet and start stomping the shredded cabbage until it was bruised enough to release most of its liquid. We got in the tub two at a time, stomped, and danced 'round and 'round while we sang a happy ditty. All done, the cabbage was salted and put into large 10 gallon stone crocks, covered with cheese cloth, and weighed down. It fermented in a few days and was ready to process into jars. Mom always made sure we had enough sauerkraut to last until the next cabbage crop. Creamed sauerkraut or sauerkraut soup was a zesty compliment to any meal.

By the end of spring, the corn began to tassel and we looked forward to eating corn on the cob. Folks with a good mastery of the English language called this corn *roasting ears*; we called it *"rozen-eers"*.

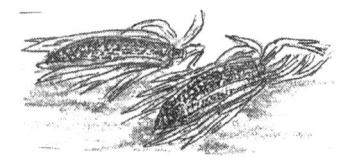

A Fine Catch!

There's not a country kid who has not experienced the fun of crawfishing. The art and skills of this fine and entertaining spring sport are best learned by hands-on experience. The city kid might find the following instructions very helpful.

"How-to Fish for Crawfish"

First, one must be able to identify the water hole that has crawfish in it. The best way to tell is by the number of mud castles on the bank indicating the presence of crawfish in the water hole. Equipment is cheap and usually easy to come by. The junk drawer in the kitchen is sure to have a three to five foot long string; a string from a feed sack or flour sack is fine. A stick, the length doesn't matter, but a limb from a Chinaberry, peach, or mesquite tree is fine and can be picked up on the way to the water hole. For bait, a left over chicken neck or a piece of bacon or *zapečene maso,* (meat preserved in lard) is fine; often it can be found in a skillet on the kitchen stove. If the meat is too fatty it's a floater and needs a sinker. Any crooked nail found in the yard and poked through it is fine. Barefooted, make your way across the pasture to the water hole. Sit down on the grassy bank, throw the baited line in the water and wait. Soon the line gets tight, pull it out on to the bank, (not too fast not too slow) and you've got yourself a fine catch! Throw the crawfish in the bucket and go for more. Some are red, some are blue, some are gray or black, but color doesn't matter, they are all fine! Don't be afraid of the crawfish, because even the wee little kids can handle them. At first they are overcome with fear when they see the threatening pinchers held high and defensively above its head, but soon learn that by placing the thumb and index finger low on its back, they can handle it just fine without getting pinched.

How to Prepare a Fine Seafood Dish

　　Clean and fry the tails, scramble a dozen eggs over them and you'll have a fine seafood dish. If too many guests show up from nowhere, you can increase the number of servings by adding another dozen eggs. In cooking this way, a few crawfish tails can feed many.

Spring Time Continues . . .

　　Spring time was for hoeing in the garden, the blackberry patch, the corn field, or the cotton patch. This was our extracurricular activity. At the end of the day, as the sun was resting on the horizon, we walked home carrying our hoe on our shoulder or used it as walking cane. Soon the hoe became a baton. Energized, we twirled as we walked, and became quite proficient twirlers. Thinking back, I wonder how come none of us ever wound up with a severed Achilles tendon?

　　Spring brightened Mom's spirit because that's when another pet project brought forth its rewards. That was her blackberry patch, for on those sticker-covered vines the promise of her tasty creations grew. Gallons and gallons of lush blackberries turned into jams, jellies, cobblers and pies.

But what a chore it was to hoe between them and later pick the berries. We were left with reminders on our hands and arms for days and days.

At the end of May, the school year was coming to an end, and as each day went by, Mother Nature was about to stop passing out the rewards of Spring. The wheel of time kept turning and each season presented new pleasures, perils and adventures.

The following is a poem I wrote and dedicated to Mother Nature, for she has been around for a very long time. She went on duty when God created the world and has stayed obedient throughout the centuries. She was here unwavering, through the 1930's and the 1940's, the good old days, and now with zest, has begun a new millennium. The world and its people are continually changing, but Mother Nature has remained constant and true. In spite of her age she has an untiring spirit, and will continue to direct and her Stars will continue to perform'til the end of time.

Beyond Ellis Island

Nature's Ballet . . . Country Style

The stage is set for a spectacular show, we're told
So folks, take your seats and watch the scenes unfold.
Featuring fares of the seasons by Stars known to all;
Summer, Winter, and Autumn (also known as Fall),
Joined by Spring, in this awesome once a year review,
Of Nature's talents, unsurpassed; no one can out-do.
This show, ordained and directed by Mother Nature,
Presents on stage, arts and skills; woes and rapture.
One by one, the Stars step up and vie for "The Best of Show."
Exhibiting color, spice, and magic, the makings of a Pro.
But years of practice and repeats do not compare
To the nostalgic '30's as I remember them, for I was there.

Curtains open to Christmas lights and Miss Winter spreading snow,
And together with Santa, making children's faces glow,
She scoops up snow for snow ice cream . . . vanilla flavor
And prepares cuisines of rabbit and wild goose, for us to savor.
With bow and arrow, plays Cupid, and on the prowl they say

Mary Betik Trojacek

To capture all the hearts in a unique and precision way.
The magic of Mardi Gras, and predictions of Ground Hog Day
Are cool events, only Miss Winter can portray.
Quilting, shucking corn, and stripping feathers;
Giving up treats for Lent .... there were no rathers.
Winter ends, curtains fall, and we blink our eyes
And Mother Nature gives the cue, for drapes again to rise.

Miss Spring makes her debut and announces, "Spring hath sprung!"
And charms us all with Larks and Robins, chirping their song.
The Lilacs and fruit trees burst out in bloom galore;
Bees humming around them, busier than ever before.
Miss Spring presents Daffodils, Pansies, and Bluebonnet hills,
And is inspired with a yen for the old crawfishing skills.
Gear in hand, and barefooted, she trod across the pasture,
Passing by newborn calves, gifts of Mother Nature.
Downy ducks, clucking hens, and baby chicks that cheep;
Easter bonnets, bunny rabbits, and colored eggs to find and keep.
With arms spread wide, she welcomes the warm and gentle

showers,
That pamper the garden peas and mother's pretty flowers.

Miss Spring takes leave, and we regret to see her go,
'Cause Miss Summer comes on, laden with chiggers and mosquito.
She shoots marbles, bats the ball, and plays with toys homemade;
No TV, no chips, no cokes; not even ice for lemonade.
A picnic, watermelon and hotdogs, on 4th of July
Honor Old Glory, as firecrackers burst and light the sky.
You see her toiling in the field, sun-up to sun-down,
Idle time is sweet and rare; no time to paint the town.
Too busy baling hay, hoeing and picking cotton,
Making haystacks, pulling corn; those days are not forgotten.
A swim in the stock pond in the dark, or in moon light
Ends her busy day with a promise of a restful night.

Miss Summer takes a bow, her time is up, her role complete
And Miss Autumn comes on stage, promising a treat.
Curtains open to pumpkins and bright falling leaves;
To the sound and sights of ducks and flying geese.

Mary Betik Trojacek

You will see her scrapping cotton and picking pecans,
Then all decked out for Halloween and the Harvest Dance.
Miss Autumn ushers kids and teachers back to school,
Respecting books, one another, and the Golden Rule.
With axe and saw, she's busy making firewood,
To warm the house in winter, and to cook our food.
She offers frosty mornings and a glorious sunset sky,
And much too soon, our "Indian Summer" is bidding us "good-bye".

The show is over, the Stars bow and smile to resounding "Encore"!
And the Director nods "Yes". They will return, like every year before
To treasure memories and hopes; and love to live each day
In kindness and thanksgiving, for the many gifts forever on display;
And to God, that He commissioned Mother Nature in this way.........
For "re-runs" sustain our life, "may we have many more", we pray!
The Stars have been so faithful year after year,
And need no prodding when it's their time to reappear.
Each performed her very best, keeping us in heart and

mind

"Just aimin' to please . . . you, and you, and you, and all mankind".

I vote "The Best of Show" to each of the Stars; plus a crown

For they are the ones who make the world go 'round.

Evelyn, ninth child of Joe and Frances Betik, born April 17, 1944.

She was baptized Evelyn Dolores. Her farm name was Evelina or Evelinka but most often we called her Linka. We older kids selected her baptismal name with no particular person in mind, so she is no one's namesake, except her patron saint. In 1964, she married Danny Slovak and they have 2 children, Darren and Sherry. Evelyn was born the same year that President F.D. Roosevelt was elected to fourth term as president of the United States. This same year, the G.I. Bill of Rights was signed into law. The rationing of meat and some other commodities had ended in the United States, but meat supplies were so low that people were eating horse meat. The year that Evelyn was born, Lillie graduated from high school, Helen was a sophomore, and I was a freshman. At this time I was having some serious thoughts about becoming a nun after I graduated from high school. I had even selected my new name . . . Sister Mary Bernadette.

War news continued to dominate the headlines. The bloodshed continued in Europe and in the Pacific, and our boys were in everyone's heart and on everyone's mind. World leaders were desperate for a solution. The Atomic bomb had been developed and its use was being considered to halt the war with Japan. Then in 1945 Allied involvement against Hitler finally began to gain ground and his defeat was seen as imminent. Hitler committed suicide April 30, 1945. A few days later Germany surrendered unconditionally. President Roosevelt did not see this glorious day, for he died April 12, 1945, just when victory was in sight. In August 1945, the use of the A-Bomb ultimately ended the war with Japan.

The Old Halls

A sense of nostalgia is associated with the old halls: the K.J.T., the Sokol, and the National Hall

1924 GRAND OPENING OF KJT AUDITORIUM, ENNIS TX

(also known as the SPJST). These fraternal lodges have been in Ennis since the turn of the century; built by Czechs on Czech foundations promoting patriotism and fellowship and providing spiritual and financial benefits. The Knights of Columbus also built a big beautiful hall. These halls have provided the atmosphere for weddings, festivals, dances and other community affairs. For many folks, going to a dance was a family function. Mom, Dad, big kids, little kids and babies all went and socialized. Admission to the dance was 25 cents for a dancing person, and the money was collected at the driveway gate. Only those persons who planned to dance had to pay. On arrival at the gate, one just had to state the number of dancing people in the car, and the rest of the carload got in free. Some of the boys just jumped the fence down the road, bypassed the gate

S.P.J.S.T. No. 25, second building, built 1923.

Fourth Sokol building. Built for approximately $7,000, plus free labor. Ten days free labor expected from every member. Opened 1936.

and saved their quarters. A quarter went a long way. They could buy five cokes or five packs of chewing gum and treat several girls during intermission.

The present day halls are of modern structure; comfortable, and spacious, and a plus for the small town of Ennis. But it's in the old halls, with their unique features, where the memories were made. Today a "Dancing Person" would have to look far and away to find a dance hall with such character as I knew one to be. Each hall had a large spacious balcony from where one could view the musicians on the stage and the people on the dance floor. There were no tables around the dance floor. Benches with backrests along the wall beneath the balcony provided comfortable seating for those who came just to listen to the music. Access to the balcony was via a stairway on each side of the front entrance. More benches were available there and everybody's Mom and Aunt, and the town "Gossipers" found the balcony the most favorite place to sit. They brought with them pillows and quilts for the little ones and laid them on the balcony floor. (Just about every family had little ones). Each hall had many windows to permit cool breezes since air conditioning was not yet available.

The dateless girls usually congregated on one side of the dance floor; the shy boys on the other, and when the band played "Paul Jones" they all rushed into the ring. Sometimes that was the only time they got to dance with the opposite gender. Girls danced with girls a lot. In high school days, Jerry and I often danced together. The lights were never turned down low; they stayed on bright the entire evening because of the many children and toddlers running around. Kids learned to dance way before they were teenagers. Some kids played tag running around among the dancers, then during intermission the dance floor was littered with kids sliding on the slick floor. There were several local musicians groups or bands that provided music for entertainment and dancing. They played the traditional Czech polkas and waltzes; however, every once in a while, they slipped in a Jitterbug or a Boogie-Woogie. The people on the floor loved it and danced away to the sounds of the new beat, but it met with disapproval from the little ladies in the balcony. That kind of music was too non-Czech. Czech people had strong feelings about their heritage and were heavy on tradition, they felt different, not better or worse, just different. They stuck together and were not accustomed to changes that veered from tradition.

Czechs married Czechs. The people, who were not of Czech descent, were called *Amerikani*. As if all of us were not Americans, including those who were verbal. It was a scandal to date an *Amerikan,* and worse yet, if you married one. Over the years even the old Czechs mellowed and accepted the changes that came along with the times. Many multi-cultural marriages followed and the traditional Czechs accepted the fact that all of us are Americans.

The little ladies in the balcony could also take notice of who was patronizing the saloon. Each hall had a saloon in the basement where beer was served and where most of the husbands could be found. It was off-limits to ladies and children, we thought, and only men were allowed there. Occasionally we did see women go through the little swinging door down the steps to the saloon and we thought ... "my, they have a lot of nerve!"

Besides balconies and saloons, the old halls had another feature in common . . . outdoor toilets. They were multiholers, and had no privacy compartments, but that didn't matter too much because there were no lights inside anyway. The toilets stood a few hundred feet behind the hall in the back of the premises. The necessary stroll, in the moonlight or in darkness, was made without fear of the Boogeyman. Inside we never saw any snakes, spiders or scorpions . . . too dark. When the new halls were built, indoor plumbing was installed, and everyone stepped up and joined the ranks of modern high society.

When I was growing up, Daddy was the only driver at our house, and when I graduated from high school, he still was the sole and only driver at our house. Therefore, when we went to church, visiting, or to a dance Daddy chauffeured us. Somehow, no one ever gave it much thought, how nice it would be if someone else could drive too. I don't remember that Daddy gave us girls too much encouragement to learn. When Daddy got his first tractor, my brother Joe soon learned how to operate it. When he got big enough to sit behind the steering wheel in the car, he craned his neck above the dashboard to look through the windshield and was rambling around on the farm. Mildred got the idea that she too wanted to ramble around, so Joe agreed to teach her. Now many years later they laugh as they relate this teaching/learning experience. Here's the scenario: Mildred gets in the car, turns on the ignition but the car won't start.

Joe, the teacher and the experienced one, gets a chain, and hooks up the car behind the old "Poppin' Johnny" tractor. He drags the car with Mildred in it, up and down the hill, over terraces, down the field road to the bottom and back, and the stubborn car never even sputtered. How frustrating!

Driver's Ed

When they returned to the yard, Daddy had a solution to their dilemma . . . the car had no battery! He had taken it out of the car and put it on the tractor.

CHAPTER XI
HIGH SCHOOL... 1943 – 1947

In the mid 40's all the little country schools that had dotted the countryside became history, as all were consolidated into the Ennis Independent School System. And with their demise, the school buses began to roll. At first they were of different colors, shapes and sizes. I remember the one we called the "cracker box"; red and white and looked like a box of crackers on wheels. It wasn't long before the bus fleet became uniform, and all the buses were painted the same identifiable pumpkin yellow. Jerry and I rode the same bus; he went to Ennis High, and I went to St. John's High.

By this time the main road, FM1181, had already been graveled for several years to down deep in Creechville, but our road to the house was a dirt road and turned into mud after a rain. Our house stood quite a way from the main road, so we had to walk down our muddy road to the bus stop. We wore an old pair of shoes or mud boots and then changed to school shoes at Trojaceks' (across the road from us). We left our muddy shoes on their front porch and boarded the bus. One day I didn't get all the mud off me and Jerry offered me his clean white handkerchief to get it cleaned off. For more than fifty years, I have remembered the kindness he extended to an embarrassed girl who was going to school with mud on the back of her legs.

When the public school buses would not transport students to private schools anymore, St. John's had to provide their own buses. Then there were two buses going down the country roads picking up school kids, but each bus was only half full. All my high school years were at St. John's. I did okay in Algebra and Chemistry, but they were not my favorite subjects. I liked science and loved Geometry. Home Economics was a fun class. One semester we cooked, the other semester we sewed. Sister Alberta taught me to crochet. Later crocheting was a pleasant way to spend a quiet, rainy, Sunday afternoon. I read lots of library books. We didn't have TV, and the loud-speaking radio didn't come to our house until about 1944. We learned about the world by reading books. Public Speaking was my worst and most stressful and dreadful subject. I was so timid; stage fright overcame me when I was asked to recite in front of the class. If confronted by one of the teachers, I got tongue tied and couldn't utter a word. Sister Marcellianus and Father Greoneger taught Religion Class. (A few years later Father Greoneger performed the marriage ceremony for Jerry and me). Whenever a good picture show with a religious theme, was being shown at the local theater, we were allowed to go to this show as part of our religion class. By the time I got out of high school, I had seen at least four movies this way. (The only ones I had ever seen) *Going My Way, Song of Bernadette, Bells of St. Mary, Fatima,* and one or two more, but they slip my mind. Many great movies were made in the '30s and the '40s that I didn't see then, but now, 50 years later as they are being resurrected and are shown on TV, I get excited and enjoy seeing them. I associate with the clothes and the hairdos of the times, the cars, and the songs, but most of all, the clean wholesomeness of the show brings a nostalgic connection to my past.

While still in high school, Jerry was working part-time at Ennis State Bank, and after he graduated in January 1947, went to work there full-time. Mr. Joe Baldridge, president of the bank, was well versed in the banking business and gave

Jerry a guiding hand. Jerry looked up to him and held him in high esteem and continued to work at the bank until July 1948 when he enlisted in the Air Force. In the 1960's, Ennis State Bank built a new facility and vacated this old landmark structure where Jerry had once worked. The old building, with the name Bank, etched on the sandstone tower is still there today and portrays a lot of history. Inside, the teller windows and the vault are still present, and in the midst of this unique setting it has been transformed into a restaurant serving Cajun cuisine to anyone yearning for the taste and flavors of Louisiana.

I have always enjoyed reading, so it's easy to understand why I liked English and Literature. I was a junior in high school when our teacher assigned each student in the literature class to write a short descriptive essay; an essay where the reader would be able to create a mental picture of the subject or scenario. I chose to write about a particular winter day on the farm. I still had a vivid picture of a scene I had observed just a few days prior to the assignment, so I decided to put this picture on paper. It went something like this:

Bird Watching

"*The ground was white, all covered with new snow that had fallen overnight. The cedar trees by the front porch were draped and laden with mounds of the white snow and the branches sagged with the unexpected weight. As the birds flitted in and out, the snow dispersed and fell to the ground in clumps and little sprinkles. The little feathered creatures appeared cold and hungry so we put out a pan of breadcrumbs on the snow-covered ground. Soon a mix of color surrounded the pan as the blue jays, the sparrows, the cardinals, the chick-a-dees, and the red-winged blackbirds, began to congregate around this feast laid out before them. Manna from heaven! Their bright colors and black beady eyes appeared even more vivid against the white snow. They chirped, and chattered, and squawked, each in his own language. Some birds were bossy and aggressive; some shy and on guard taking refuge in the protective branches of the cedar trees nearby and waiting for an opportunity to steal a crumb. The blue jays were the most greedy.*" I found the activity of the birds quite entertaining and I associated their behavior with people.

I thought I presented a pretty good description of a scene captured when bird watching. I turned my paper in and I couldn't believe I got an "F" grade. No questions asked. I was told I had copied it out of a book and it was not acceptable. I was too timid and shy to protest or explain and too embarrassed for the class to know, so I just crumbled it and threw it in trash.

Father Micola, pastor of St. John Church and superintendent of the school was a very intelligent person and one of his many talents was he organized and directed the school band. I joined the band and played the clarinet, but soon found out that I was not going to set the world on fire as a musician.

Bobby . . . chartered Baby-Boomer.

Bobby, the last of the ten, was born October 07, 1946. He was baptized Bohumil Anthony. On the farm we called him Babik; his school name was Bobby, in the business world he is known as Bob. Simply by association of the birth year, Bobby connects with Hollywood because Liza Minnelli shares his birth year. This same year IBM introduced its first electronic calculator. In 1946 the rationing of butter, shoes, and tires, came to an end in the USA, while in Britain, bread rationing had just begun. The world was picking up the pieces after W.W.II. The G.I.'s were coming home, the economy began to boom, and so did the baby population.

The babies born in this post-war era were, and still are, referred to as Baby Boomers. This year also saw the height of the Polio Epidemic (Infantile Paralysis), and public health officials and families watched with anxiety and apprehension as it took its toll. Mostly young people and children were stricken. Many were dying or were left crippled. The victims whose respiratory system had been paralyzed were put in the Iron Lung. The Iron Lung was a large metal tube with port holes to administer to the needs of the patient while maintaining the right pressure to support his breathing. It was used quite extensively when I was in nursing school, but is antiquated now. Modern technology has advanced to the state of the art respirators, called ventilators by professionals.

When Bobby was born, there were ten of us living in this three-room house on our home-place. Lillie was the only one who had left the nest. Then, with each passing year or so, another graduated from high school and struck out on their own and then family numbers began to decrease and the house didn't seem as crowded.

Bobby Anthony Betik married Barbara Ann Bakluda, and their initials were, and are B.A.B. They had two children born to them: Beverly Ann (Lincks) and Bart Anthony. They

Mary Betik Trojacek

too were B.A.B.'s.

I was a senior when Bobby was born. Such a close connection to a newborn baby caused me to have deep thoughts about God's creation and how it all fit into His plan. And there was our English teacher back in action again, encouraging the students in Literature class, to enter a national essay contest, sponsored by the Extension Magazine, a national magazine published monthly for teens. Bobby was only a few weeks old and I had such profound thoughts about the miracle of birth, I chose to write about Bobby. My essay won honorable mention and was published in the national magazine. I kept the little write-up and tucked it away in a box of mementos. Years later I came across it, and as I read it, I found myself awed by some of the profound words and phrases I had used. In reading it, I realized how appreciation for the gift of life only deepens with the passing of time. Having experienced childbirth with my own children, I have true respect for God's plan, purpose and miracles.

The second half of my senior year, the Nuns had the students to focus on careers. I was undecided as to what I wanted to do after I graduated, but back of my mind I was still thinking about becoming a Nun. During Career Week, Sister Macaria asked the class to write down their ideas on careers. The first thoughts that entered my mind came from seeing ads on posters, billboards, and in magazines, portraying nurses in the Army and the Navy. Throughout the war years Uncle Sam advertised heavily to recruit nurses for the military, even set up programs to train women in the Cadet Nurse Corp. In each advertisement were the words "Career" and "Nurse" and they seemed to go hand in hand. So, I wrote about nursing as a career, even though I really knew nothing about it. Sister Macaria took these "career papers" written by the students, and went about contacting sources to obtain scholarships and sponsors to further the education of her graduates. A few weeks later, Sister informed me that I had been given a full 3-year scholarship to St. Paul Hospital School of Nursing. The scholarship came from the Dallas Women's Chamber of Commerce and included tuition, room and board, my uniforms and laundry, my books, and any required fees. I was pleased and happy about it because now I had a direction of which way to go.

In summary, there was nothing dramatic or very exciting about my high school days. I went with the flow. I was plain, shy, and reserved, and never had a date. But people often told me I had a pretty smile. So I smiled a lot. I graduated from St. John's High School in May 1947, and stayed home that summer to help Mom and Dad get the cotton crop in. Classes at St. Paul Hospital School of Nursing were to start February 21, 1948. I was about to venture out into a world of push button gizmos and gadgets. This was so different from pure country where we still had no indoor plumbing, electricity, or telephone.

The year 1947 was the year of my high school graduation and was also the year that Princess Elizabeth and Prince Philip got married in England. The world had not yet recovered after the war, and food shortages continued in war-torn Europe. The United States was sending vast amounts of supplies, grains, and money to ease the crisis and help the people to put their lives back together.

I lost my senior class ring even before I graduated from high school. I "planted" it somewhere in the homeplace orchard while I was hoeing between the fruit trees (probably the cursed white grass). My class ring had cost $18.75 and I had bought it with my hard-earned cotton-picking money.

1948 A year of Important decisions:
   Helen gets married.
   I enter School of Nursing.
   Jerry enlists in U.S. Air Force.

My sister Helen and Bill Barrett were married February 7, 1948. This day was a typical winter day, cold and raining. Daddy had parked the car at the road the day before the rain came because we knew our road would be impassable. Getting to the car that morning was the same way we always did after a rain. We walked to the road in an old pair of shoes or mud boots and then changed to Sunday shoes. Helen, the bride, was privileged this day; she did not have to walk in the mud. Clutching her wedding dress and bridal attire in a box, she rode on Old Red, the family horse, while my little brother Joe, reins in hand, led them to the waiting car. My brother Joe, age 13, remembers leading Old Red down the muddy road and jokingly says he felt like he was St. Joseph leading the donkey with the Virgin Mary astride going to Bethlehem. Upon arriving at the church, Helen went to the Sisters Convent and changed into her wedding dress. Bill met her at St. John's Church and the wedding proceeded on schedule. I was her only attendant and Bill's friend was Best Man. It was a quiet wedding without fanfare; no big dinner or dance.

Two weeks from this day I was due on campus at St. Paul Hospital School of Nursing, Dallas, Texas. I was 18 years old, anxious and excited, for now I had a sense of direction and I knew what I was going to do. Even though I liked Jerry a lot, we had never had a date. There didn't seem to be much hope or promise for a relationship, so I stopped thinking about him and concentrated on my goal of becoming a Registered Nurse. In July of 1948 (four-and-a-half-months after I was settled at St. Paul), Jerry enlisted in the U.S. Air Force. Shortly before his enlistment we made a connection and an unspoken commitment, heart and soul, was born!

CHAPTER XII
CONCLUSION

The dreams of Joe and Frances Betik had reached their peak and then as the years went by, sadly began to wane. When Daddy was putting his last crop in, sometimes he would mention how bad he felt on that day. He said he got off the tractor just to lie down on the ground until the pain subsided. When he planted the 1967 crop, it was with the intention that it would be the last; that he would retire and do the things he wanted to do. And as fate would have it, this was his last crop. Before it was even harvested, he began to feel ill. We could see his health failing, and it was not long before he was diagnosed with Lymph-sarcoma. Mr. Trpak and neighbors finished gathering the crop for Daddy. In January 1968 he was admitted to St. Paul Hospital in Dallas, where he stayed for more than two months, too ill to go home. Mom stayed with him day and night. He longed to go home and see his faithful dog, Rex, and his cows. If he could see them just one more time, it would have filled a void. In his isolated world of pain and agony, it would have given him a quiet and peaceful closure in his resignation to the will of

God, but they never saw each other again. The cancer took its toll rapidly, and claimed Daddy's life March 13, 1968. I believe this has been the deepest regret of my life: he was denied his last wish on this earth. We all knew he was terminally ill, and I wish that arrangements could have been pursued to take him home, control his pain, keep him as comfortable as possible, and grant him his last wish to see Rex and his cows again and just let him die at his home. That's the way he would have wanted it to be, but we were all clinging to false hope and praying for a miracle. My heart aches and my eyes well up in tears. (Note: If the world of Hospice as we know it today could be taken back in time to 1968, I believe that he would have been granted his last wish). Daddy deserved that. He was such a good man and worked so hard for his family all his life.

After Daddy passed away, Mom lived on the homeplace alone for a while but was not able to run the farm. Arthritis degenerated her hip joints and hip replacement became necessary. She gave each of her ten children an opportunity to buy the farm, but by this time, each one was up to their ears in responsibilities with their own homes and families and did not want to add extra burden on themselves.

Some of her children now have regrets that the home-place did not stay in the family. Mom sold the farm to Gardner and Ople Parker and she bought a house in town close to church. This house, at 606 S. Kaufman had belonged to her sister, Anna Kosarek. After Mom moved there, the house became alive with activity. Her back door was always open and children, grandchildren, and friends dropped in frequently. Sundays after church, it looked like an early morning party was going on as family came after Mass to visit with Mom. And she always had food to offer; cobbler, donuts, chicken noodle soup, or strudel. This was the mark of a gracious Czech host.

Living close to church gave her comfort, and her flowers and garden-spot pleasure. Often the Nuns would come to her house and pick a bouquet of flowers for the altar. She had a little vegetable garden which she tended and called it her physical therapy. She lived alone and managed her own affairs; her dogs kept her company. First it was Pancho, followed by Nikki. In 1988, Mom suffered a stroke and was in need of greater care than could be provided for her in her home, so she became a resident at a local nursing home. She seemed to be content where she was but her health was failing and she passed away January 09, 1991.

Mom and Dad had realized their dream of owning their own land and worked so hard to preserve it. They put in twenty-five years of hard labor and sweat to have a very productive farm. Daddy was putting his crops in with crude farm equipment and a team of mules. They terraced the land to conserve the soil. They fought the Johnson grass to improve their crop yields and converted nonproductive acres to good use. Mom worked in the fields too, relentlessly, even when she was expecting a child; she hoed, picked cotton, and performed other tasks, up until it was time to have her baby. Now that their farming days are over and gone forever, I drive by the home-place, their beloved farm, and see that it has been enclosed in pasture, that the Johnson grass is flourishing again from one boundary to the other, and mesquite trees have taken over the cotton land. I reflect on my Mom and Dad, and how much this farm had meant to them. As I reflect, I have a vision, and in this vision I see my Mom and Dad in the fields working sun-up to sun-down. They have that sparkle in their eyes and the will in their minds and motions, because this is their land. But I can see the stress and wear on their tired and weary bodies, and with sadness I say to myself, "all their sweat and toil has been for naught." Rest in peace, *Maminko a Tatinku*.

I brush away a tear and look for justification. I ponder over all that had transpired and all that had been accomplished on this farm that Mom and Dad called their land and we kids called our home-place. While the seeds of cotton and corn were planted into the ground year after year, Mom and Dad also planted seeds of honesty, integrity, self-discipline, and self-sufficiency in their children. They cultivated these values and molded their sons and daughters to be what they are today. They taught them how to work, instilled in them respect for fellow man, and inspired them with the spirit and magic of laughter.

Lots of water has run down the Creechville hills to the *nižina*, the lowland that once fostered a dream. The water is long gone, but the memories remain, and will not float away with the passing of time. I found it very interesting writing about my childhood and reminiscing over the memories I had collected over so many years. With amazing clarity one little flash of memory just brought something else to my mind; it was like one little door just opened another, however, I don't think all the doors were opened. I know this to be so, because when my brothers, sisters, and cousins get together and conversation drifts from the present into the past my memory cells get jogged with tales of what had slipped away from me. Amid laughter and nonsense as stories about episodes of the past are told, a fog is lifted and another dormant incident is brought to life. "Oh, I remember that!" There's a common thread that binds all of us connecting our present to the past, and there would not be a present as we know it, if it had not been for our past. Years ago, our destiny was formed and a legacy was born. In the process of this writing my wish is to perpetuate this legacy to the next generation, with the hope that it brings them understanding and an appreciation of the early immigrants who made all of this possible. A century has passed since so many immigrants first viewed America from Ellis Island, Galveston, or other ports of entry. What I have written is not especially unique to my family alone because all of us, being descendants of immigrants, lived under the circumstances and the life style of the times and everyone has his own interesting stories to tell. This is my story, and I hope that you will find *"Beyond Ellis Island"* interesting, informative, and entertaining, "for that's the way it was."

Today, in our world of plenty, if anyone thinks life isn't fair, that working conditions are uncomfortable or that just rewards have passed him by, take a moment and think of my Mom and Dad, or your own Mom and Dad, or ancestors who lived through hard times, perhaps even think of trading places with them. You will have an attitude adjustment that will make you want to say, "My cup runneth over."

I have no regrets about the way I grew up. Mom and Dad gave all they had. It was not Utopia, but our life was honest, clean, happy and wholesome. It made me what I am, and I like being Me. If the family values of the 1930's and the 1940's would have been carried over into the millennium, perhaps more people today would count their blessings and respect the golden rule and fewer people would feel the need to lock their doors and put bars on their windows.

Many years ago I found an article in a newspaper written anonymously by one who lived in the 1930's and the 1940's. I found it fitting because I too can relate to that era. I saved it and I think it has merit to be included here. A well-grounded sense of historical perspective is portrayed in this article. I was awed by the changes that have occurred in front of my very eyes in the years that followed the '40's. Living in the second half of the twentieth century and witnessing such profound and mind-boggling changes and developments, scares my mind and shakes my soul.

"Survivors of the '40s should rejoice.................."
"For all those people born before 1940, congratulations. We are survivors. Consider the changes we have witnessed:
We were born before television, cellophane tape, digital clocks, Frisbees, frozen food, Xerox, contact lenses, penicillin, polio vaccine and the pill.
We were growing up before radar, microwave ovens, electronic music, credit cards, split atoms, laser beams, ballpoint pens, punk rock and pet rocks; before dishwashers, clothes dryers, and panty hose. Women wore nylons.
Men walked on the moon only in the Buck Rogers comic strip. We got married first and then lived together. How quaint can you be?
In our time, closets were for clothes, not for coming out of. Bunnies were baby rabbits and rabbits were not Volkswagen; designer jeans were scheming girls named Jean or Jeanne.
Having a meaningful relationship meant getting along with our

cousins. We thought that fast food was what you ate during Lent; pressure was what was in the pressure cooker when the peas sprayed all over the ceiling. Outer space was the back of the local theater.

We were before house-husbands, gay rights, computer dating, dual careers and computer marriages. We were out of grammar school before the invention of day-care centers, group therapy, and nursing homes.

An emergency room was a place in the hospital where we went when we were too sick, or too badly injured for the doctor to take care of it in the office. We never heard of FM radio, tape decks, electric typewriters, word processors, artificial hearts or yogurt.

The only guys who wore earrings were pirates in the movies. For us, time sharing meant togetherness, not computers or condominiums; a chip was a piece of wood. Hardware was hard ware, the stuff we bought in wonderfully acrid-smelling stores with oiled wooden floors. Software wasn't even a word.

We associated the smell of burning leaves with autumn, and the smell of mothballs with winter woolens. In 1940, "Made in Japan" meant junk and the term "making out" referred to how we did on exams. Pizza, McDonald's, Gray Panthers, instant coffee and Boy George were unheard of.

Cher was a French term of endearment; we knew that because Maurice Chevalier told us so. We hit the scene when there were five and ten cent stores, where you bought things for a nickel or a dime.

Ice cream cones were five cents; double dip with sprinkles were ten cents. For one nickel, you could ride a trolley, make a phone call, purchase a Pepsi or Nehi, or buy enough stamps to mail one letter and two postcards. And, they'd arrive on time.

You could have a Chevy-coupe for $600, but who could afford one? A pity, too, because gasoline was only 11 cents a gallon. In our day, cigarette smoking was fashionable; a good meal was based on meat with potatoes and gravy.

Grass was mowed (by hand), not smoked, Coke was a cold drink not an epidemic; and pot was what you boiled the Thanksgiving turkey-bones in to make soup.

A leveraged buy-out was how the biggest kid in the neighborhood traded baseball cards. Folk music was

Grandma's lullaby.

AIDS were helpers in the principal's office. You knew the minute a Gene Kelly moving picture was released because all the high-school kids started wearing white socks and loafers.

We certainly were not born before the difference in the sexes was discovered, but we surely preceded sex-change operations, breast augmentation and fragrances for men. We made do with what we had.

And we were the last generation that was so dumb as to think you needed a husband to have baby. No wonder there's a generation gap today".

Author....... Unknown

ISBN 1412035511-1

Made in the USA
Middletown, DE
09 December 2019